Tuscan FOOD & FOLKLORE

Jeni Wright

LAUREL
GLEN

Publishing Director: Laura Bamford

Senior Editor: Sasha Judelson
Assistant Editor: Katey Day
Commissioning Editor: Nicola Hill

Art Director: Keith Martin
Senior Designer: Louise Leffler
Designers: Louise Griffiths and Les Needham

Production Controller: Dawn Mitchell

Photographer: Peter Myers
Home Economist: Annie Nichols
Stylist: Penny Markham
Picture Researcher: Claire Gouldstone
Indexer: Ann Barrett

Acknowledgments
Front and back jacket flaps (background image),
back jacket background : Joe Cornish
Front and back jacket flap top—Reed International
Books
Front jacket—Reed International Books
Back jacket inset—Reed International Books
Back jacket flap bottom, front cover on cloth under
jacket—Hulton Getty Picture Collection
Reed International Books Ltd : 3, 4, 7, 33, 82, 94, 124
Robert Harding Picture Library:
Philippe Roye/Explorer 28, /Mike Newton 104,
/Adam Woolfitt 78
Hulton Getty Picture Collection: 1 drop-in, 9, 10, 20,
25, 41, 46, 51, 61, 75, 108, 111, 115
Caroline Jones: 1 main pic, 5, 6, 8, 68
Tony Stone Images: Joe Cornish 36, /Sepp Dietrich 64

Tuscan Food and Folklore
Jeni Wright

Published in the United States by
Laurel Glen Publishing, 1997.

Laurel Glen Publishing
5880 Oberlin Drive, Suite 400, San Diego, CA 92121

First published in 1997 by Hamlyn
an imprint of Reed International Books Limited
Michelin House, 81 Fulham Road, London SW3 6RB
and Auckland, Melbourne, Singapore and Toronto

ISBN 1-57145-628-7
Library of Congress Cataloging-in-Publication Data
available upon request.

Printed in China

For Fritz, with love and thanks

*E un particolare ringraziamento a Elisa Surini e Monica
Merli par il loro prezioso aiuto*

NOTES

All recipes serve 4 unless otherwise stated

*Standard level spoon measurements are used in all recipes.
1 tablespoon = one 15 ml spoon
1 teaspoon = one 5 ml spoon*

Eggs should be medium unless otherwise stated.

Milk should be full fat unless otherwise stated.

*Fresh herbs should be used unless otherwise stated. If unavailable use
dried herbs as an alternative, but halve the quantities stated.*

*Ovens should be preheated to the specified temperature—if using a fan-
assisted convection oven, follow the manufacturer's instructions for
adjusting the time and temperature.*

Contents

introduction

Meet an Italian away from home, and one of the first things he will tell you is the village, town, or region where he was born: this will always be more important to him, more deep-rooted, than his sense of national pride. He will forever feel he is a Milanese or a Florentine, before being an Italian.

This basic characteristic is more than evident in the cuisine of Italy, for it is the regions that have given the country its national dishes. It may be said that Italy has a native, but not a national cuisine—*la cucina Italiana* is derived directly from *la cucina regionale*.

An Italian will always remain unshakable in his belief that his regional cuisine is, quite simply, the best, and Tuscans are no exception to this rule. One of Italy's most rural regions, Tuscany thrives on a wealth of outdoor markets, small groceries, butchers, and specialty food stores; here every cook is prepared to make a journey each day to buy fresh ingredients for the family meal.

THE ETRUSCANS

Cooking as homecraft, as a source of pride, goes back further in time in Tuscany than in any other region in Italy.

From the 8th to the beginning of the 5th century BC, the Etruscans grafted their civilization on a region stretching from the Alban hills down as far as Rome. Much about them still remains a mystery—their language has never been deciphered, and because they built mainly in wood rather than stone, there is little that remains to give a complete picture of their lives, unlike the way that the Romans are chronicled.

What we do know is that the Etruscans were a people close to the land, undoubtedly attracted by the beauty of this lush green region; its gentle springs and winters, its hot summers with fields strewed with flowers. They planted and cultivated with care, cleared forests and built towns, and drained the marshes of Maremma along the coast.

This part of Tuscany still evokes a heavy atmosphere of mystery today, and is steeped in many legends and myths that add to the mystique of the early Etruscan settlers.

"The long-nosed, sensitive-footed, subtly-smiling Etruscans, who made so little noise outside the cypress groves."
D.H. Lawrence
Cypresses

We also know from tombs and temples that the Etruscans were a very spiritual people, involved in the wonder of nature in all its aspects. The seasons were symbolic of the whole process of life and death, and death was accepted as a new beginning.

Tomb paintings show how they celebrated death as an occasion to be marked by a banquet with dancing. They also show how much pleasure the Etruscans derived from eating and drinking, and how they lived life to the full and hunted for pleasure as well as food. There is evidence that banquets, dancing, and festivities played a regular and important part in their lives and, in fact, it is possible that too much of *la dolce vita* was a reason for their demise.

The Etruscan custom of eating well and sharing the occasion with family, friends, and servants has contributed to the shaping of the Tuscan— and Italian—attitude to food, its cultivation and enjoyment. Yet the Etruscans did not integrate well with the local people, and this aloofness and superiority is regarded as typically Tuscan. The people of Tuscany are very different in character, even from their close neighbors in Umbria.

"I was astounded to see these peasants in Tuscany with a lute in their hands, and at their side the shepherds reciting Aristo by heart."
Montaigne
Journal du Voyage en Italie

THE RENAISSANCE

By the time of the Renaissance, some of the town and village communities that the Etruscans had established had grown into beautiful and influential cities —Siena, Lucca, Pisa, and Florence—and the region was home to a long list of celebrated artists and scholars, among them Lippi, Botticelli, Leonardo da Vinci, and Michelangelo.

Florence was the center of fine Italian gastronomy at this time, and the ruling Medici dynasty was famous for its extravagant banquets. The tradition reached its peak in 1469 when Lorenzo de' Medici celebrated his wedding for a full three days and provided guests with five royal banquets.

In the 16th century, the *Compagnia del Paiolo*, Italy's first academy of cooking comprising the twelve best chefs, was founded in Florence; and it was Caterina de' Medici who was credited with passing the art of fine cooking on to the French. When she married the Dauphin in 1533, she took a team of Florentine chefs with her to France. They made an immediate impact at court banquets with their lavish desserts and pastries, and to this day the influence of Italian pastry chefs can be seen in French *pâtisserie*.

At the same time that the wealthy merchants in Florence were enjoying sumptuous banquets, there remained in the region the tradition of passing on culinary arts and attitudes to the lower classes. Ingredients were available to the peasants in the countryside as much as to the nobility, and tables throughout the whole region were graced with game birds, mushrooms and truffles, and a huge range of vegetables that either grew wild or had been cultivated since Etruscan times.

THE RAW INGREDIENTS

Tuscan food is sometimes criticized for its simplicity, for being too plain. Tuscans would argue that their regional cuisine is simple because they have eliminated what is not essential—their region produces ingredients that in themselves are of such high quality they need little or no embellishment. Tuscan cooking is simple and unsophisticated, rooted in the countryside and determined by the seasons.

The quality of the locally produced olive oil cannot be questioned. Its production in local mills was started by the Etruscans thousands of years ago. The very best olive oil, some say in the whole of Italy, is the first cold pressing—or extra-virgin oil—from Lucca. It is produced in many parts of the region by methods little changed over the centuries. The harvest is collected by hand, and each of the farmers bring their crops to the local mill, where they stay and watch each stage of milling

and pressing until the oil reaches the bottle.

The distinctive, huge, big-horned Chiana cattle that are reared locally give the region one of its most famous dishes, *lombatina alla fiorentina*. The meat is simply cooked over an open fire, then brushed with olive oil just before serving.

Chiana beef has become world renowned, like its natural partner Chianti, one of Italy's finest and most famous wines.

"Florentines who eat beans lick their plates and tablecloths."
Traditional Saying

The neighboring Umbrians were the first to give the Tuscans their nickname of *mangiafagioli*—the bean-eaters —a result of so many of their dishes having dried beans as their main ingredient. In olden times, the traditional method of preparing them was *al fiasco*—the beans were immersed in water and olive oil in a Chianti flask. The flasks were then carried by the laborers to the fields, kept cool in the stream during the day, then cooked overnight in the embers of the wood fire that had cooked the evening meal. Beans then became the first meal of the next day.

One of the oldest Tuscan dishes, *la ribollita*, is a soup that combines the two staple ingredients of traditional peasant cuisine, bread and beans, while *acquacotta*—literally "cooked water"—is a simple vegetable soup poured over slices of stale bread before serving. Both of these soups are still served in many Tuscan homes during the winter months.

The bread of the region—*schiacciata*—is very distinctive. It is a flat, round, country bread, and is traditionally marked on the top with the baker's initials. It contains no salt, and therefore goes stale very quickly; hence it is frequently used in soups. *Schiacciata* tastes especially good with the local salty prosciutto, which is produced from Tuscan corn-fed pork and is then marinated in salt and garlic.

Bruschetta is known throughout Italy, but the Tuscan version, known locally as *fettunta*, is often not toasted, but simply a thick slice of stale bread soaked in superior extra-virgin olive oil.

For generations Tuscan children have been raised on *pappa al olio*—this is a slice of bread rubbed with garlic; the bread is then coated in olive oil and water. This has traditionally been a baby's first meal, and is still a supper time favorite with older children.

is accompanied by a huge banquet: *feste* in Tuscany have always meant food. The celebration dinner before the Palio is thought to bring good luck to all its contestants; traditionally no visitor is refused a seat at the table.

THE FESTIVALS

Tuscans have a unique pride in their heritage, and a real sense of their own history. Small village folk museums celebrate local history and local crafts rather than the grandeur of the Renaissance or the greatness of its culture. Local history is celebrated by locals reenacting scenes from the past, such as the Joust of the Saracen in Arezzo, and the famous Palio in Siena in July and August. Each festival event

Many of the region's *feste* are purely a celebration of food itself. These are known as s*agre*, celebrations to give thanks for the local harvest or for nature providing a particular delicacy, whether it be hedgerow thistles or bread for soup. One local *festa* that dates back to Roman times is the *sagra delle lumache*, held each spring in Cavriglia, in honor of the local snail crop. The local people enjoy a private harvest in April,

collecting the firm, juicy snails immediately after a shower of rain. For the *sagra* itself, preparation for the feast takes well over a week, and thousands of snails are gathered and marinated for five days before being served, forty to fifty per person.

The first big celebrations of the year are the *carnivale* before Lent. Even in small villages there will be a masked ball, an excuse to eat and drink and celebrate the "farewell to flesh." Easter marks the beginning of the *festa* season proper, and from May until the end of September there will not be a weekend in Tuscany when one of the old hilltop towns will not be celebrating in style. Easter itself is an important event in the Christian calendar, but it is steeped in traditions that have their roots in Etruscan times. In most Tuscan villages, when spring cleaning the home has been done and the mattresses have been turned, the local priest visits each family to bless a bowl of eggs. This was originally a tribute to the egg as a symbol of the never-ending circle of life and death, and the egg was a favorite symbol on Etruscan tombs, where men are seen at their death banquet holding an egg between thumb and forefinger.

It is Easter when egg dishes are served. Especially popular are the flat omelettes, *frittate* and *tortini*, which are often cut into small pieces and served as part of an antipasto.

Around this time, many families plant their garden vegetables, and in local communities there is a superstition about the time when this planting should be done. It is the same superstition associated with the picking of mushrooms and herbs: according to Tuscan folklore, this should be under a *luna calente*—after the full moon, just as it is beginning to wane.

Mushrooms are picked with similar care and due ceremony in September. It takes considerable skill to sift out the inedible mushrooms from the succulent, tasty, edible *funghi* that grow in this region.

The most sought after are the large, firm *porcini* which grow around the oak and chestnut trees. The best specimens have firm enough flesh to be grilled over open wood fires; those of less good quality are stewed or cooked in soups and risottos.

Around the same time, whole villages turn out to collect chestnuts. The area around Lucca is famous for its large, plump *marroni*, which in olden days were used to make flour for bread and polenta. One of the last *sagre* of the year is at Pontremoli near Lucca, where the harvest is celebrated with pancakes made from ground chestnut flour, filled with the local white Romano-type cheese. This was considered excellent food for new mothers, a time when they should eat only *in bianco*

—"in white"—food such as rice, pasta, Romano, and ricotta cheeses.

By September, *la caccia*—the hunting season—is in full swing. The hunting traditions established by the Etruscans live on in this region, and the quality and flavor of the local game is superb. The pheasants, larks, and thrushes live on woodland berries that give them a distinctive flavor; in true Tuscan tradition they are cooked and served simply. One of the high spots of the hunting season is the *Sagra del Tordo*, or Festival of the Thrush, which takes place in Montalcino on the last Sunday in October. Charcoal-grilled thrush is the local specialty, together with roast suckling pig, or *porchetta*.

Come November, around All-Saints Day, *la caccia* turns to big game, and the hunt goes on for wild boar, which centuries ago first provided the meat for the coarse and salty prosciutto hams that are so much favored in Tuscany.

The last *feste* of the year start on the Sunday before Christmas, traditionally a time for cooking at home and entertaining the family. In Tuscany, this means simple meals with homemade tagliatelle and tortellini, and on Christmas Eve, ravioli stuffed with spinach.

Christmas would not be complete without *panforte*, the confection which has been made in Siena since the Middle Ages. *Pan pepato* and *panforte di Siena* are flat cakes flavored with a mixture of nuts, fruit, spices, and honey. *Panforte* is more famous, less peppery, and a little sweeter than *pan pepato*. Legend has it that *panforte* was created as a gift for the Christ Child by a young Tuscan boy who had nothing to give other than what was in his pocket—a stale piece of bread and some nuts which he encrusted into the bread with some honey.

After Christmas meals, *panforte* is eaten with *vin santo*, a dessert wine made by a traditional process requiring the pressed grapes to be matured in tiny barrels in attics for 4 or 5 years. *Vin santo* is enjoyed at other times with *cantucci*—hard biscuits made especially for dunking into sweet wine.

The beauty of Tuscany is apparent throughout the year.

The climate is as welcoming as its people, and the two combine with the landscape to give the region a unique charm that has been the source of inspiration to artists and writers throughout the ages. It is Tuscany's romantic atmosphere, just as much as its fine art and architecture, that attracted Byron, Shelley, the Barrett Brownings—and later D. H. Lawrence, one of Tuscany's most ardent admirers.

Their Etruscan ancestors handed down to the Tuscans an appreciation of food and wine, which was passed on to their neighbors and children. The dedication to simplicity in the preparation of food, the appreciation of the quality of raw natural ingredients, and the pleasure of enjoying food have, over time, been passed on to the whole of Italy.

antipasti
& soups

Antipasti are served at the beginning of lunch and dinner, as appetizers. For everyday family meals, this is usually just one or two tasty tidbits—a simple *bruschetta* or *crostini*, a slice or two of salami or *prosciutto*, and maybe a few olives or preserved vegetables. Salads are more popular when the meal is more of an occasion, and on the coast grilled and charbroiled shellfish are a specialty, but antipasti are rarely elaborate in Tuscany.

Soup is served as a first course, *primo piatto*, as an alternative to rice or pasta. It depends on the meal, but many Tuscan soups are chunky, based on beans, vegetables, and bread. They are hearty, substantial, and warming, and can make complete meals in themselves.

Country Bread with Olive Oil & Garlic
Bruschetta

4 large slices of country bread

2 fat garlic cloves, halved

8 tablespoons extra-virgin olive oil

coarse sea or rock salt

This very simple antipasto is traditionally made with sourdough bread at olive harvest time in late autumn. Bruschetta is its best-known name outside of Tuscany, but locally it is also called fettunta.

1 Toast the bread on both sides under a preheated broiler until light golden. While the bread is warm, rub one side with the cut side of the garlic.

2 Put the bread on a plate and drizzle 2 tablespoons of olive oil over each slice. Sprinkle with salt to taste and serve immediately.

Cook's Notes

To match the flavor of the first pressing of Tuscan olives, use the best extra-virgin olive oil you can afford, and check the label to ensure that it is from the first cold pressing. The fruity, green olive oil from Lucca is said to be one of the best (see page 6).

Tuscans like to toast their bread over an open fire—the word bruschetta comes from bruscare, *meaning "roast over coals." You can do this too, or you could charbroil it on a cast-iron broiler pan on top of the stove. Look for a close-textured bread such as* pugliese—*it is better for bruschetta than the open-textured ciabatta.*

Serves 2–4
Preparation time: 10 minutes

*"The city lies along the ample vale,
Cathedral, tower and palace, piazza and street,
The river trailing like a silver cord
Through all."*

Elizabeth Barrett Browning
writing about Florence

Tuna & Bean Salad
Tonno e Fagioli

½ lb. dried cannellini beans,
soaked (see Cook's Notes)

6 tablespoons extra-virgin olive oil

3 tablespoons lemon juice

7 oz. can tuna in olive oil,
drained and flaked

2 heaped tablespoons finely
chopped flat-leaf parsley

1 small red onion, sliced into thin
rings

salt and pepper

Few people realize that this popular Italian dish comes from Tuscany, because it can be seen on trattorie *menus everywhere. The authentic Tuscan version always uses red onions.*

1 Drain the beans and rinse under cold running water. Put them in a large saucepan, cover with fresh cold water, and bring to a boil. Boil rapidly for 10 minutes; then lower the heat and half cover with a lid. Simmer for 2 hours or until the beans are tender, skimming off the scum and adding water as necessary.

2 Drain the beans thoroughly in a colander, then pour them into a large bowl.

3 Whisk together the oil and lemon juice, season with salt and pepper to taste, and pour over the warm beans. Stir to coat the beans in the dressing, then leave to cool.

4 Fold the tuna and parsley into the cold beans and taste for seasoning. Chill in the refrigerator until ready to serve.

5 Just before serving, stir the beans and taste for seasoning again, then top with the red onion rings.

Cook's Notes

To soak dried cannellini beans, put them in a large bowl and cover with plenty of cold water. Cover and leave to soak at room temperature overnight. For a quick-soak method, put the dried beans in a large saucepan, cover with plenty of cold water, and bring to a boil. Boil rapidly for 10 minutes, then cover with a lid, remove from the heat and leave to soak for 3–4 hours.

Look for tuna canned in olive oil in Italian delicatessens. Although more expensive, it is far superior to the tuna canned in vegetable oil or brine which you find in most supermarkets.

When the dressing is added to the beans while they are still warm, it soaks into them and gives them more flavor. If you are short of time use a 15 or 16 oz. can of beans; drain and rinse them well before use, and heat them through quickly before adding the dressing.

Serves 4

Preparation time: 20 minutes, plus overnight soaking and chilling
Cooking time: 2¼ hours

Pancakes with Spinach & Ricotta
Crespelle alla Fiorentina

1 Make the tomato sauce: heat the oil in a saucepan, add the shallot, carrot, celery, and garlic and cook gently, stirring, for 5 minutes until softened. Add the passata, stock, and basil and season to taste. Bring to a boil, cover, and simmer for 30 minutes.

2 Make the pancakes: sift the flour and a pinch of salt into a bowl and make a well in the center. Add the eggs; gradually whisk in the milk and draw the flour in from the sides to make a smooth batter.

3 Moisten a paper towel with oil and wipe it over the inside of a 7 inch nonstick crêpe pan. Heat until hot. Swirl in a ladleful of batter and cook for 1–2 minutes until bubbles appear on the underneath and the pancake comes away from the side of the pan. Turn the pancake over and cook for 1–2 minutes longer. Slide the pancake out of the pan so that the first side is facing upwards. Repeat to make 12 pancakes, wiping the pan with oil as necessary, and stacking the pancakes up, with waxed paper between them.

4 Stir the parsley into the tomato sauce and spread half of the sauce over the bottom of a large baking dish. Mix together the ingredients for the filling, and add salt and pepper to taste. Put ½ of the filling on one of the pancakes, spooning it down one side, then roll the pancake up around it. Place the pancake in the baking dish and then repeat with each pancake. Pour over the remaining tomato sauce.

5 Make the béchamel sauce: melt the butter in a saucepan, add the flour and cook gently, stirring, for 1–2 minutes until golden. Gradually whisk in the milk and bring to a boil. Simmer for 2–3 minutes until thickened, whisking to keep it smooth. Remove from the heat, stir in half of the Parmesan, then season to taste.

6 Pour the béchamel over the tomato sauce, sprinkle with the remaining Parmesan and bake in a preheated oven at 350°F for 30–35 minutes. Serve hot, straight from the dish.

Cook's Notes
The amount of batter for the pancakes is very generous because the first few pancakes are not always perfect. If you are lucky, you can make 16–20 pancakes out of this amount of batter.

Serves 6
Preparation time: 1 hour
Cooking time: 30–35 minutes

TOMATO SAUCE:
2 tablespoons olive oil
1 shallot, finely chopped
1 carrot, finely chopped
1 celery stalk, finely chopped
1 garlic clove, crushed

3 cups passata (tomato sauce)
1 cup vegetable stock or water
1 teaspoon dried basil
2 tablespoons chopped flat-leaf parsley
salt and pepper

PANCAKES:
2 cups flour
2 eggs, beaten
2½ cups milk
sunflower oil, for frying

FILLING:
8 oz. ricotta cheese
4 oz. frozen chopped spinach, defrosted and well drained
2 eggs, beaten
1 tablespoon grated Parmesan cheese
pinch of grated nutmeg

BECHAMEL SAUCE:
¼ cup (1 stick) butter
2 tablespoons flour
2¼ cups milk
2 oz. Parmesan cheese, grated

Tomato & Bread Salad

Panzanella

4 thick slices of country bread
(*pane di campagna*)

1 red onion, finely chopped

1 large garlic clove, finely chopped

½ cucumber, skinned and diced

¼ cup plus 2½ tablespoons
    extra-virgin olive oil

2 tablespoons red wine vinegar

4 ripe Italian plum tomatoes,
    roughly chopped

a small handful of flat-leaf parsley,
    roughly chopped

a small handful of basil leaves

salt and pepper

TO GARNISH (OPTIONAL):

1 oz. arugula

1 oz. radicchio

Traditionally panzanella was a way for frugal cooks to use up stale country bread, but now it has become quite a fashionable antipasto or primo piatto in its own right. It is a salad for days when tomatoes are at their sweetest.

1 Tear the bread into a large salad bowl. Add the onion, garlic, and cucumber and stir well to mix.

2 Whisk together the oil and vinegar and season with salt and pepper to taste; pour onto the salad and toss to mix. Leave to stand at room temperature for at least 30 minutes.

3 Add the tomatoes and parsley to the salad, then tear the basil leaves into the bowl. Toss to mix, then taste for seasoning. Serve at room temperature, garnished with arugula and radicchio if desired.

Cook's Notes

You can vary the vegetables according to what is freshest and best at the time. Peppers can be used instead of cucumber, and arugula instead of basil.

Serves 4
Preparation time: 20 minutes, plus 30 minutes standing

"At the Café Procacci in Florence the proprietor makes a purée of white truffles which, made into little sandwiches, goes down particularly well at eleven o'clock in the morning with a glass of good white Tuscan wine."

Elizabeth David,
Tuscan Food

Broiled Mussels
Cozze Gratinate

10 cups (4 pints) mussels

¾ cup plus 2 tablespoons white wine

½ red pepper, deseeded and chopped

2 garlic cloves, crushed

4 tablespoons finely chopped parsley

I lb. can tomatoes, drained and chopped

5 tablespoons fresh white breadcrumbs

2 tablespoons olive oil

I tablespoon grated Parmesan cheese

salt and pepper

1 Put the mussels in a large bowl, cover them with cold water and discard any that are open, cracked, or rise to the top. Scrub them well under cold running water to remove any barnacles and the beards. Put the cleaned mussels in a large saucepan with the wine and bring to a boil, covered with a closely fitting lid.

2 Reduce the heat and cook the mussels for a few minutes, still covered, shaking the pan occasionally until the mussels open. Discard any mussels that do not open. Remove the open mussels from the pan and remove and throw away the top half of each shell.

3 In a bowl, mix together the chopped pepper, garlic, parsley, chopped tomatoes, and 4 tablespoons of the breadcrumbs. Stir in 1 tablespoon of the olive oil and then season to taste with a little salt and some pepper.

4 Add a little of this mixture to each of the mussels in their shells and place them in an ovenproof dish. Sprinkle with grated Parmesan and the remaining breadcrumbs and olive oil and bake in a preheated oven at 450°F for 10 minutes. Flash the mussels under a preheated hot broiler for a crisp top. Serve immediately.

Serves 4–6
Preparation time: 30 minutes
Cooking time: 10 minutes

*"Whose bread and cheese I eat,
to his tune I dance."*

Florentine Saying

Mixed Vegetable Soup
Minestrone di Verdura

1 Place the navy beans in a large bowl and cover them with water. Leave them to soak for 8 hours or overnight. Drain the beans and then rinse under cold running water.

2 Heat the oil in a large pan and add the onions, garlic, and bacon. Sauté gently for 5 minutes, stirring occasionally, until soft and golden brown.

3 Add the beans, 7½ cups water, herbs, and tomatoes, cover the pan and simmer gently for 2 hours. Add the carrots and simmer for 10 minutes. Stir in the potatoes and turnip and cook for 10 minutes.

4 Add the celery and cabbage to the soup with the pasta and cook for 10 minutes, or until the pasta and vegetables are tender. Add the parsley and season to taste. Stir in half the Parmesan and ladle the soup into bowls. Serve immediately, sprinkled with the remaining Parmesan.

Serves 6
Preparation time: 20 minutes, plus overnight soaking
Cooking time: 2½ hours

¼ lb. dried navy beans

3 tablespoons olive oil

2 onions, chopped

2 garlic cloves, crushed

3 bacon slices, chopped

1 teaspoon chopped marjoram

½ teaspoon chopped thyme

4 tomatoes, skinned and chopped

2 carrots, diced

2 potatoes, diced

1 small turnip, diced

1–2 celery stalks, chopped

8 oz. cabbage, shredded

2 oz. small pasta shapes

1 tablespoon chopped parsley

5 tablespoons grated Parmesan cheese

salt and pepper

Chicory Soup
Zuppa Delicata di Insalata Riccia

1 Heat 4 tablespoons of the butter in a pan over low heat, add the onion, and fry until golden. Add the chicory and cook slowly in the butter for 10 minutes, then season with salt and pepper to taste. Pour in the wine, and when this has evaporated, stir in most of the milk and the stock. Bring slowly to a boil. Mix the corn flour with the remaining milk and add to the pan; stir constantly to avoid lumps.

2 Cook for 25 minutes over medium heat, then whisk in the grated Parmesan cheese and the remaining butter, cut into pieces.

3 Toast the stale bread in a preheated oven at 400°F for about 10 minutes until golden brown. Place the toast in warm soup bowls and pour the soup over. Serve hot.

Serves 4
Preparation time: 5 minutes
Cooking time: 55 minutes

6 tablespoons butter

1 onion, diced

2 chicory heads, finely chopped

¼ cup dry white wine

1¾ pints milk

1 chicken bouillon cube, dissolved in 1 cup boiling water

2 tablespoons corn flour (available in health food stores)

2 tablespoons grated Parmesan cheese

8 slices of stale bread, buttered

salt and pepper

Tasty Bean Soup
Crema di Fagioli Saporita

¾ lb dried navy beans

1 carrot, chopped

1 onion, quartered

1 bouquet garni

4 oz. cooked smoked ham, cubed

3 tablespoons butter

2 shallots, finely chopped

1 garlic clove, crushed

1 tablespoon chopped parsley

salt and pepper

4 oz. croutons, to serve

1 Soak the beans overnight in cold water and drain.

2 Place the beans in a large pan with 3½ pints water and bring to a boil over medium heat. Boil for 1½ hours or until the beans are just tender. Add the carrot, onion, bouquet garni, and the cubed ham and simmer for 20–30 minutes. Place the soup in a blender or food processor, but be sure to remove the bouquet garni first. Purée until smooth. Return the purée to the pan and reheat over medium heat.

3 Melt the butter in a heavy-based pan and gently fry the chopped shallots and garlic until golden but not brown. Add the chopped parsley and mix together quickly. Add the shallot mixture to the bean purée.

4 Mix well with a wooden spoon, season well with salt and pepper, then pour into bowls. Sprinkle with croutons and serve hot.

Serves 4
Preparation time: 30 minutes, plus overnight soaking
Cooking time: 2¼ hours

Pumpkin Soup
Minestra di Zucca

4 lb. pumpkin

2 tablespoons olive oil

1 tablespoon butter

1 onion, roughly chopped

2 large garlic cloves, roughly chopped

2 old potatoes, roughly chopped

5 cups chicken stock

¼ teaspoon ground cinnamon

½ cup heavy cream

salt and pepper

olive oil, to serve

This autumn soup is superbly smooth and creamy, and the orange-fleshed pumpkin makes it the most wonderful, warming color.

1 Cut the pumpkin into quarters or eighths. Scrape out and discard the seeds and fibers, then peel the pumpkin pieces and roughly chop the flesh.

2 Heat the oil and butter in a large heavy saucepan until foaming. Add the onion and cook gently, stirring frequently, for about 5 minutes until softened but not colored. Add the chopped pumpkin flesh, garlic, and potatoes and cook gently, stirring frequently, for another 5 minutes.

3 Pour in the stock, add the cinnamon, season with salt and pepper to taste, and bring to a boil. Half cover and simmer gently for 30 minutes or until the vegetables are very soft.

4 Pour the soup in batches into a food processor or blender and process until smooth, then return to the pan. Add the cream and reheat, stirring frequently; then add water to thin down the consistency if necessary. Taste for seasoning.

5 Pour into warmed bowls, drizzle with olive oil, and grind black pepper over the top. Serve immediately.

Cook's Notes
Pumpkin is a member of the squash family, a group of vegetable fruits that is harvested in summer and autumn. Although bland in flavor, squash have the perfect soft texture for soup making, and they take on the flavor of other ingredients very well. Other suitable types of squash for this recipe are zucchini and summer squash, and acorn and butternut squash. You will only need about 2 lbs. of any of these, because there is less waste than on a pumpkin.

Serves 4–6
Preparation time: 20 minutes
Cooking time: 30 minutes

Fava Bean & Artichoke Soup
Minestra di Fave, Cicorino e Carciofi

1 Remove the skins from the fava beans. Clean the artichokes, then wash and remove any coarse outer leaves.
2 Heat the oil in a deep pan over low heat, add the onion and cook for about 4 minutes until golden. Add ½ cup of the stock and leave to simmer for 4 minutes.
3 Add the fava beans and artichokes, mix well and cook for 5 minutes. Add the potatoes and chicory to the pan, then cover with the remaining stock and bring to a boil. Simmer for 45 minutes. Remove the potato, mash, and return to the soup.
4 Beat the egg yolks in a soup tureen with the cream, Parmesan, and parsley. Season with salt and pepper. Gently add the soup, then quickly stir to mix. Serve hot, with croutons.

Serves 4
Preparation time: 10 minutes
Cooking time: 1 hour

8 oz. podded fava beans

3 artichokes

3 tablespoons olive oil

½ onion, finely chopped

6¼ cups vegetable stock

2 large potatoes, peeled and thickly sliced

1 chicory head, sliced thinly

2 egg yolks

2 tablespoons light cream

2 tablespoons grated Parmesan cheese

½ oz. parsley, chopped

salt and pepper

4 oz. croutons, to serve

Country Rice Soup
Minestra di Riso alla Rustica

1 Heat 2 tablespoons of the oil in a large pan over low heat, add the onion, leeks, sausages, and potatoes and cook for 10 minutes.
2 Mix the bouillon cubes with 6¼ cups water and pour into the pan. Simmer over medium heat for 30 minutes.
3 Rinse the spinach in cold water, remove the stalks and any damaged leaves. Cook in a pan with only the water clinging to the leaves and a pinch of salt, for 4–5 minutes. Drain and squeeze out any excess moisture. Chop finely and add to the soup.
4 Bring to a boil, add the rice, mix well and simmer for about 10 minutes until the rice is tender. Add the cheese, a sprinkling of pepper, and the remaining oil. Mix well before serving.

Serves 4
Preparation time: 10 minutes
Cooking time: 55 minutes

3 tablespoons olive oil

1 onion, finely sliced

3 leeks, finely sliced

¼ lb. Italian sausages, skinned and crumbled

2 potatoes, peeled and cubed

2 vegetable bouillon cubes

12 oz. fresh spinach

5 oz. long-grain white rice

2 tablespoons grated Romano cheese

salt and pepper

Mushroom Soup
Acquacotta con Funghi

7 tablespoons olive oil

2 garlic cloves, crushed

1 lb. field mushrooms, sliced

8 oz. tomatoes, skinned and
   chopped

3½ cups vegetable stock

6 large slices of hot toasted bread,
   cut into quarters

2½ oz. Parmesan cheese, grated

2 eggs, beaten

salt and pepper

1 Heat the oil in a heavy pan. Add the garlic and fry gently until it begins to brown. Add the mushrooms and cook for 5 minutes, stirring frequently. Add the tomatoes and stock and season to taste. Bring to a boil, then lower the heat, cover and simmer for 15 minutes.

2 Divide the toast slices between 6 bowls, then sprinkle with about half of the Parmesan. Mix the eggs with the remaining Parmesan and add to the soup mixture in the pan. Remove from the heat immediately and stir vigorously. Pour the soup over the toast and serve immediately.

Serves 6
Preparation time: 5 minutes
Cooking time: 25 minutes

Potato Soup with Parsley
Minestra di Patate e Pressemolo

6¼ cups beef stock

4 potatoes, peeled and coarsely
   grated

1 egg yolk

1 hard-boiled egg yolk, mashed

¼ cup light cream

2 oz. Parmesan cheese, grated

1 tablespoon finely chopped
   parsley

salt and pepper

4 oz. croutons, to serve

1 Place the stock in a pan and bring to a boil. Sprinkle the potatoes with salt and pepper and then drop into the boiling stock. Cook for about 15 minutes, stirring from time to time.

2 Beat the egg yolk in a soup tureen and add the mashed hard-boiled egg yolk. Blend the cream, Parmesan, and finely chopped parsley into the egg mixture and whisk them together.

3 Carefully pour 1 cup of the stock into the egg mixture. Reheat the remaining stock and potatoes and gradually add them to the soup tureen. Sprinkle with croutons and serve warm.

Serves 4
Preparation time: 10 minutes
Cooking time: 20 minutes

Lentil Soup
Zuppa di Lenticchie

Warming lentil soup is a quintessential winter dish. Tuscans eat it as a first course, either for lunch or dinner, whichever is the main meal of the day. It is such a hearty soup that it could make a satisfying dish on its own, served with chunks of crusty country bread and followed by cheese and fruit.

1 Heat the oil and butter in a large heavy saucepan until foaming. Add the onion and carrot and cook gently, stirring frequently, for about 5 minutes until softened.

2 Add the lentils and garlic and stir well to mix, then pour in the stock and bring to a boil. Add the tomato purée, stir until it is thoroughly mixed into the liquid, then add the marjoram and salt and pepper to taste. Half cover and simmer gently for 30 minutes.

3 Pour half of the soup into a food processor or blender and process until smooth, then return to the pan of soup and stir to mix. Add water to thin the consistency if necessary, then taste for seasoning. Serve hot, sprinkled with fresh marjoram leaves and grated Parmesan.

2 tablespoons olive oil

1 tablespoon butter

1 large onion, finely chopped

1 large carrot, finely chopped

6 oz. brown continental lentils

1–2 garlic cloves, crushed

2 quarts chicken stock

2 tablespoons tomato purée

1 teaspoon dried marjoram

salt and pepper

TO SERVE:

marjoram leaves

freshly grated Parmesan cheese

Cook's Notes

There are many different kinds of lentils, and they range in color from yellow to orange, red, green, and brown. In Italy, brown lentils are used, and you will find them in packages at any Italian delicatessen, or at the supermarket—sometimes labeled "continental lentils." They have an earthy flavor and nutty texture, and tend to hold their shape in cooking better than the orange and red types. Like all lentils, they do not need to be soaked before cooking.

Serves 4–6
Preparation time: 15 minutes
Cooking time: 30 minutes

Bean & Cabbage Soup
La Ribollita

8 oz. dried cannellini beans, soaked in cold water overnight

6 tablespoons olive oil

2 onions, roughly chopped

2 carrots, thickly sliced into rounds

2 celery stalks, roughly chopped

2 potatoes, roughly chopped

4 tablespoons passata (tomato sauce)

8 oz. Savoy cabbage, finely shredded

pinch each of dried rosemary and thyme

4 oz. stale white bread, crusts removed

salt and pepper

This is one of Tuscany's most famous soups. The name "ribollita" means re-boiled, and refers to the fact that in the old days the soup was reheated and served day after day. To make it stretch further when there was little meat and vegetables to spare, bread was added. In honor of this tradition, bread is now included in the soup when it is first made.

1 Drain the beans and rinse under cold running water. Put them in a large saucepan, cover with fresh cold water, and bring to a boil. Boil rapidly for 10 minutes, then lower the heat and half cover with a lid. Simmer for 1½ hours or until the beans are tender, skimming off the scum and adding water as necessary.

2 Transfer about half of the beans and liquid to a blender or food processor and process until smooth.

3 Heat 4 tablespoons of the oil in a saucepan, add the vegetables and cook gently, stirring frequently, for 10 minutes until softened.

4 Add the passata and puréed beans and stir well to mix, then add the cabbage, 4 cups of water, the herbs, and salt and pepper to taste. Bring to a boil, then cover and simmer gently for 1 hour.

5 Tear the bread into the soup and add the whole beans and their liquid. Stir well to mix, then simmer for 10 minutes longer. Taste for seasoning. Serve hot, drizzled with the remaining oil.

Cook's Notes
The Savoy cabbage can be replaced with any other leafy green of your choice, such as spinach, sorrel, or spring greens. Sometimes leeks are included, and even a ham bone—there are no hard-and-fast rules.

Some versions of this soup are served au gratin—*with a thick crust of sliced onions and Parmesan cheese on top. This is a good way of serving it in individual bowls, like a French onion soup. Ladle the soup into heatproof bowls, sprinkle with finely sliced onions and grated Parmesan, and bake in a preheated oven at 350°F for 30 minutes.*

This soup is excellent reheated and served the next day. The beans and bread thicken on standing, so add some water when reheating. Fresh leaves can be added, or another green vegetable, such as peas or green beans.

Serves 6
Preparation time: 20 minutes, plus overnight soaking
Cooking time: 2½ hours

Tomato Soup with Croutons
Pappa al Pomodoro

4 tablespoons olive oil

1 onion, chopped

3 garlic cloves, crushed

1½ lb. tomatoes, skinned and chopped

4½ cups chicken stock

8 oz. stale bread, crusts removed, diced

a few basil leaves, chopped

salt and pepper

1 Heat half the oil in a large pan, add the onion and garlic, and fry gently for 4–6 minutes until golden but not brown. Add the tomatoes and cook for 5 minutes, then gradually stir in the stock. Add salt and pepper to taste, then simmer for 30 minutes.
2 Meanwhile, heat the remaining oil in a skillet, add the bread cubes and fry, turning, until crisp and golden.
3 Add the basil and croutons to the soup and serve immediately.

Serves 4
Preparation time: 5 minutes
Cooking time: 40 minutes

Wild Mushroom Soup
Zuppa di Porcini

In spring and autumn, one of the great Tuscan pastimes is to hunt wild mushrooms in the woods. Mushroom gatherers return home with baskets full of edible fungi, and this is the time to make soup.

1 Trim off the woody ends of the mushroom stems and discard. Chop the mushrooms.

2 Heat the oil and butter in a large heavy saucepan until foaming. Add the onion and cook gently, stirring frequently, for about 5 minutes until softened but not colored. Add the mushrooms and garlic and stir to mix with the onion, then sprinkle in the flour and stir over low heat for 1–2 minutes.

3 Gradually pour in the stock, stirring all the time; then bring to a boil, and add salt and pepper to taste. Half cover and simmer gently for 20 minutes.

4 Stir in the mint and taste for seasoning. Serve hot.

Cook's Notes

Porcini *are the type of wild mushrooms suitable for this soup. Literally translated,* porcini *means "little pigs," and these delicious wild mushrooms are so called because of their bulbous, fat shape. They are* boletus edulis, *known as* cèpes *in French, and can be found in the woods in this country, but it is dangerous to gather wild mushrooms unless you are an expert on the subject or are with someone who is.* Porcini *can be bought at most grocery stores and supermarkets, but they are expensive, so to cut the cost you can use half* porcini *and half cultivated button mushrooms. Another alternative is to buy a few dried* porcini *and use these in conjunction with both wild and cultivated mushrooms to simulate the flavor. Dried* porcini *are highly concentrated and intensely "mushroomy," so a little goes a long way. For instructions on how to use them, see the recipe for Wild Mushroom Risotto on page 40.*

In Tuscany, a type of wild mint called mentuccia *is used, but ordinary garden mint can be substituted.*

Serves 4

Preparation time: 20 minutes
Cooking time: 20 minutes

12 oz. fresh wild mushrooms (see Cook's Notes)

2 tablespoons olive oil

1 tablespoon butter

1 onion, roughly chopped

1 large garlic clove, roughly chopped

1 tablespoon flour

5 cups beef stock

2 teaspoons chopped mint (see Cook's Notes)

salt and pepper

Zucchini Soup with Basil

Zuppa di Zucchine al Basilico

4 tablespoons olive oil

2 tablespoons butter, softened

I large onion, finely chopped

I½ lb. zucchini, sliced

2 potatoes, peeled and diced

6¼ cups chicken stock

12 fresh basil leaves, chopped finely

I garlic clove, chopped finely

2 eggs

I oz. Parmesan cheese, grated

salt and pepper

TO SERVE:

6 slices of crusty bread

grated Parmesan cheese (optional)

1 Heat the oil and 1 tablespoon of the butter in a heavy deep pan. Fry the chopped onion in the oil and butter over low heat until golden, but not brown.

2 Add the sliced zucchini, mix well and fry over low heat for about 10 minutes.

3 Add the diced potatoes to the pan and stir over medium heat for 3–4 minutes before adding the chicken stock. Bring to a boil slowly, cover the pan with a lid and simmer over medium heat for 40 minutes. Purée the soup in a blender or food processor to obtain a smooth mixture.

4 Place the basil in a bowl with the garlic, eggs, remaining softened butter, and the Parmesan, then beat with a wooden spoon or whisk. Trickle the soup into the beaten egg mixture and season with salt and pepper. Return the soup to the pan and then reheat gently over low heat.

5 Place a slice of crusty bread on the bottom of each soup bowl and pour the hot soup over it. Serve immediately, sprinkled with grated Parmesan if desired.

Serves 6
Preparation time: 15 minutes
Cooking time: 1 hour

Grandmother's Soup
Minestra della Nonna

1 onion

2 leeks

2 tablespoons oil

2 tablespoons butter

12 oz. pumpkin flesh, cubed

7 oz. canned plum tomatoes

6¼ cups hot vegetable stock

5 oz. rice

1 tablespoon chopped parsley

3 oz. Parmesan cheese, grated

salt and pepper

1 Chop the onion coarsely with the white parts of the leeks. Heat the oil and butter in a large deep pan and cook the onion and leeks over low heat for 4–6 minutes until golden, but not browned. Add the cubed pumpkin, mix with a wooden spoon, and leave to cook over low heat for another 10 minutes.

2 Mash the tomatoes with a fork and add them to the pan. Stir well and cook for 10 minutes, then season with salt and pepper to taste. Pour in the hot stock and simmer for 30 minutes.

3 Bring the soup to a boil, then sprinkle in the rice. Reduce the heat and simmer until the rice is just tender, then add the chopped parsley and half the Parmesan.

4 Mix the soup well and pour it into a warm soup tureen. Serve sprinkled with the remaining Parmesan.

Serves 4
Preparation time: 10 minutes
Cooking time: 1 hour

Hunter's Soup
Minestra del Cacciatore

5 oz. ground veal

1 egg

2 oz. cheese, grated

2 tablespoons butter, melted

¼ teaspoon grated nutmeg

4½ cups beef stock

salt

grated Parmesan cheese, to serve

1 Mix the veal with the egg in a bowl. Add the grated cheese, melted butter, a pinch of salt, and the nutmeg.

2 Work the ingredients together until well mixed, then form into firm balls, about the size of walnuts, in the palms of your hands.

3 Heat the stock until boiling, then add the veal balls and cook over high heat for 15 minutes.

4 Serve the soup hot, sprinkled with grated Parmesan.

Serves 4
Preparation time: 5 minutes
Cooking time: 15 minutes

Chicken Soup
Ginestrata

1 Mix together the egg yolks, stock, Marsala, and cinnamon. Pass the liquid mixture through a fine strainer into a pan. Cook gently until hot, stirring constantly, then add the pieces of butter and continue stirring until the soup thickens. Pour the soup into warmed soup bowls and sprinkle with the sugar and nutmeg. Serve immediately.

Serves 4
Preparation time: 5 minutes
Cooking time: 10 minutes

4 egg yolks

2¼ cups chicken stock

1¼ cups dry Marsala wine

pinch of ground cinnamon

6 tablespoons butter, diced

3 tablespoons sugar

pinch of grated nutmeg

Sweet Red Pepper Soup

Acquacotta con Peperoni

4 tablespoons olive oil

I red onion, finely chopped

2 celery stalks, thinly sliced

2 red peppers, cored, deseeded, and cut into very thin strips

2 plum tomatoes, roughly chopped

I garlic clove, crushed

I tablespoon flour

1¾ pints chicken or vegetable stock or water

I teaspoon sugar

2 eggs

4 thick slices of country bread

salt and pepper

chopped flat-leaf parsley, to garnish (optional)

Acquacotta means "cooked water," a traditional soup that takes its name from the days when it included little more than a few vegetables boiled in water and poured over slices of stale bread. In olden times it was daily fare for the poor charcoal burners working in the Tuscan woods, but nowadays there are many versions of acquacotta made rich with different vegetables, eggs, and Parmesan cheese. This recipe, and Acquacotta con Funghi (see page 24), are typically modern.

1 Heat the oil in a large heavy saucepan; add the onion, celery, and red peppers and cook gently, stirring frequently, for about 10 minutes until softened.

2 Add the tomatoes, garlic, and flour and stir well to mix. Cook for 1–2 minutes, stirring, then pour in the stock and bring to a boil. Add the sugar and salt and pepper to taste, half cover and simmer gently for 30 minutes.

3 Whisk the eggs in a bowl with salt and pepper to taste, then whisk in a ladleful or two of the hot soup. Pour this mixture into the pan of soup and heat very gently without boiling, stirring all the time. Taste for seasoning.

4 Put a slice of bread in the bottom of 4 soup plates, ladle the soup over and garnish with parsley, if using. Serve hot.

Cook's Notes

Although not traditional, this soup is very good puréed, without the bread. Cook it for 40 minutes or until the peppers are very soft, process until smooth in a blender or food processor, then thicken with the eggs. If you like a very smooth consistency, force the soup through a strainer to remove the pepper skins.

Serves 4

Preparation time: 15 minutes
Cooking time: 30 minutes

rice dishes

Tuscans are big bread eaters, but they also love rice, especially risotto. It is usually served as a first course, *primo piatto*, on its own, before the main course of fish or meat. Sometimes it is plain and simple, just rice cooked in water or stock, with maybe some fresh herbs or a splash or two of wine. Other times it is made more substantial and colorful, cooked with vegetables, seafood, or meat. Traditionally, risotto is served in small portions in large wide-rimmed soup plates, topped with Parmesan or Romano. Once upon a time these cheeses were always grated, but nowadays they are often shaved into curls.

Sage Risotto
Risotto alla Salvia

4½ cups vegetable stock

2 tablespoons olive oil

2 tablespoons butter

1 shallot, finely chopped

12 oz. arborio rice

¼ cup dry white wine

20 fresh sage leaves, finely chopped

2 tablespoons light cream

1 oz. Gruyère cheese, grated

salt and pepper

a few sage sprigs, to garnish

1 Warm the stock in a pan over very low heat and gradually bring to a boil. Heat the oil and butter in a large pan and add the shallot. Fry over medium heat for about 4 minutes until golden but not brown. Gradually add the rice, stir well, and continue to cook for a few minutes.

2 Add the wine and simmer until it has completely evaporated, then add the boiling stock a little at a time and cook, stirring frequently for about 25 minutes, until the stock has all been absorbed and the rice is creamy. Taste and season if necessary.

3 At the end of the cooking time, add the sage leaves, cream, and Gruyère cheese. Turn off the heat, cover and leave to rest for a few minutes before serving, garnished with sage.

Serves 4
Preparation time: 5 minutes
Cooking time: 35–40 minutes

*"Young girl that in the field hast work begun,
And with thy great straw hat dost seem the Sun,
Fair thief-of-hearts they call thee, every one."*

Folk Rhyme

Wild Mushroom Risotto

Risotto di Porcini

3 tablespoons butter

4 oz. fresh wild mushrooms, soaked (see Cook's Notes), and thinly sliced

2 garlic cloves, crushed

½ oz. dried wild mushrooms (see Cook's Notes)

2 tablespoons olive oil

1 onion, finely chopped

10 oz. arborio rice

½ cup dry white wine

about 5 cups boiling chicken stock

salt and pepper

finely chopped flat-leaf parsley, to garnish

A risotto is one of the best dishes for using a small quantity of precious wild mushrooms. The rice helps "stretch" the mushrooms to feed more people.

1 Melt 2 tablespoons of the butter in a pan, add the fresh mushrooms and half the garlic, and cook over low heat, stirring frequently, for about 5 minutes until softened. Remove from the heat and set aside.

2 Remove the dried mushrooms from the soaking water with your hands and squeeze them over the bowl to press out as much liquid as possible. Strain the liquid to remove grit, then reserve. Chop the mushrooms very finely.

3 Heat the oil and remaining butter in a casserole or saucepan until foaming. Add the onion and cook gently, stirring for 5 minutes until softened but not colored. Add the soaked mushrooms and remaining garlic and cook, stirring, for another few minutes.

4 Add the rice and stir until the grains start to burst, then add the wine and stir until the sizzling stops.

5 Add the mushroom soaking liquid and about ¼ of the hot stock and cook over moderate heat, stirring frequently, until all the stock is absorbed. Add salt and pepper to taste and repeat with the remaining stock, adding it about ¼ at a time and stirring, until the rice is creamy. The consistency should be almost soupy.

6 Reheat the fresh mushrooms over high heat, then add to the risotto and fold in gently. Taste and adjust seasoning, if necessary. Serve immediately in warmed soup plates, sprinkled with parsley.

Cook's Notes

Any fresh wild mushroom will taste good in risotto, but porcini (boletus edulis) *are the most commonly used.*

Dried wild mushrooms are available in packages from supermarkets; Italian delicatessens also sell them loose. Although they may seem expensive, their flavor is very strong, so they are only used in very small quantities. Before use, they must be reconstituted. Put them in a bowl, cover with warm water, and leave them to soak for 20–30 minutes.

Serves 4

Preparation time: 15 minutes, plus soaking
Cooking time: 25–30 minutes

Country-style Risotto
Risotto alla Rustica

1 Heat the oil and all but 1 teaspoon of the butter in a large pan over low heat, then add the vegetables, herbs, and garlic. Simmer the vegetable and garlic mixture for 5 minutes over medium heat, stirring occasionally.

2 Sprinkle in the rice, allow it to turn golden. Moisten with the wine and simmer until the liquid evaporates. Add the plum tomatoes, mashing with a fork.

3 Mix well and continue to cook by stirring and gradually adding the boiling stock, for about 25 minutes until the stock has been absorbed and the rice is tender. Taste and adjust the seasoning, if necessary.

4 As the rice becomes creamy, add the reserved butter and plenty of pepper. Stir in the cream just before serving.

Serves 4
Preparation time: 5 minutes
Cooking time: 35–40 minutes

2 tablespoons olive oil

3 tablespoons butter

2 shallots, finely chopped

I small onion, finely chopped

I sprig of rosemary, finely chopped

I tablespoon finely chopped parsley

¼ teaspoon finely chopped marjoram

4 basil leaves, finely chopped

I garlic clove, crushed

12 oz. arborio rice

¼ cup dry white wine

4 plum tomatoes, peeled

1¾ cups boiling vegetable stock

2 tablespoons light cream

salt and pepper

Risotto with Sweet Pepper & Eggplant
Risotto con Peperoni e Melanzane

2 tablespoons olive oil

3 tablespoons butter

I shallot, finely chopped

I eggplant, finely chopped

I red pepper, cored, deseeded, and finely diced

4½ cups vegetable stock

12 oz. arborio rice

¼ cup dry white wine

I tablespoon chopped parsley

4 basil leaves, finely chopped

I oz. Parmesan cheese, grated

2 tablespoons light cream

salt and pepper

1 Heat the oil and all but 1 tablespoon of the butter in a deep pan. Add the shallot and fry over medium heat for a few minutes until golden, but not brown. Add the eggplant to the pan with the diced pepper. Cook for about 5 minutes on fairly high heat. Meanwhile put the stock in another pan over medium heat and slowly bring to a boil.

2 Add the rice to the vegetable mixture, stir for a few minutes, then add the wine. When this has evaporated, pour in a little of the boiling stock. Continue adding stock, stirring frequently, for about 25 minutes, until the rice is creamy and the stock has been absorbed.

3 Taste and adjust the seasoning, if necessary. Add the remaining butter, chopped herbs, Parmesan, and cream. Mix well and serve.

Serves 4
Preparation time: 5–10 minutes
Cooking time: 30 minutes

Risotto with Meat
Risotto alla Fiorentina

2 tablespoons olive oil

5 tablespoons butter, softened

I onion, sliced

½ lb. ground beef

¼ lb. kidneys, sliced

I chicken liver, sliced

13 oz. tomatoes, skinned and mashed

13 oz. arborio rice

4½ cups boiling beef stock

3 oz. Parmesan cheese, grated

salt and pepper

1 Heat the oil and half the butter in a heavy pan; add the onion, and fry gently for 5 minutes until golden. Add the ground beef, kidneys, and chicken liver; increase the heat and fry until browned, stirring. Add the tomatoes and season to taste; lower the heat and cook for 30 minutes.

2 Stir in the rice, then add half the stock. Cook for 20–25 minutes, stirring and adding the remaining stock to moisten, as necessary.

3 When all the liquid has been absorbed and the rice is creamy, remove from the heat. Stir in the remaining butter and the Parmesan and fold gently to mix. Leave to stand for 2 minutes, then serve.

Serves 4–6
Preparation time: 10 minutes
Cooking time: about 1 hour

Seafood Risotto
Risotto alla Marinara

1 Scrub the mussels thoroughly under cold running water to remove any barnacles and the beards, and discard any that are open or cracked. Put the cleaned mussels in a large saucepan with a little water, and boil, covered with a closely fitting lid, until they open. Shake the pan occasionally. Strain and set aside, retaining the cooking liquid. Discard any mussels which do not open.

2 Heat the olive oil in a large deep skillet. Add the onion and garlic and fry gently until soft and golden, stirring occasionally.

3 Stir in the rice and cook over low heat for 1–2 minutes, stirring until the grains are glistening with oil and almost translucent. Pour in some of the fish stock and the reserved mussel liquid and wine, and bring to a boil.

4 Meanwhile, soak the saffron in a little boiling water and add to the risotto with the prepared shrimps, scallops, and squid. Reduce the heat to a simmer and cook gently, stirring frequently and adding more fish stock as necessary, until the rice is tender and creamy and all the liquid has been absorbed. This will take about 25 minutes. Stir in the mussels and season with salt and pepper to taste. Sprinkle with parsley and garnish with oregano.

Serves 4–6
Preparation time: 25 minutes
Cooking time: 45 minutes

I pint fresh mussels in their shells

4 tablespoons olive oil

I onion, chopped

2 garlic cloves, crushed

12 oz. arborio rice

7½ cups boiling fish stock

½ cup dry white wine

a few strands of saffron

¾ lb. peeled, cooked shrimps

½ lb. scallops, sliced

½ lb. prepared squid rings

2 tablespoons chopped parsley

salt and pepper

sprigs of fresh oregano, to garnish

"The Etruscans shared the banqueting bench with their wives, which is more than the Greeks or Romans did, at this period. The classic world thought it indecent for an honest woman to recline as the men did, even at the family table. If the woman appeared at all, she must sit up straight, in a chair."

D.H. Lawrence
Etruscan Places

Rice with Fontina & Gorgonzola
Riso con Fontina e Gorgonzola

12 oz. arborio rice

¾ pint milk

1 tablespoon butter

3 tablespoons flour

5 oz. Gorgonzola cheese, diced

¾ cup light cream

5 oz. Fontina cheese, rind removed, and diced

salt and pepper

1 Boil the rice in salted water, according to the package instructions. Drain well.

2 Put the milk in a small pan over low heat.

3 Soften 2 tablespoons of the butter in a pan; add the flour, stirring well, then gradually add the hot milk, stirring continuously to make a sauce. Gradually add the small pieces of Gorgonzola and season with salt and pepper. Remove from the heat and stir in the cream.

4 Place the drained rice in a bowl with the diced Fontina cheese and mix with the remaining butter.

5 Using ⅓ of the rice, make a layer of rice in a buttered ovenproof dish; cover with ⅓ of the Gorgonzola sauce. Repeat the layers with the remaining ingredients, making 2 further layers.

6 Place the dish in a preheated oven at 350°F for 10 minutes, then serve immediately. For best results the rice needs to be very hot, but the sauce on top should not brown.

Serves 4
Preparation time: 10 minutes
Cooking time: 35 minutes

"From Tuscan Bellosguardo,
Where Galileo stood at nights to take
The vision of the stars, we have found it hard,
Gazing upon the earth and heavens, to make
A choice of beauty."

Elizabeth Barrett Browning
Complete Verse

pasta

Tuscany is not known for its pasta dishes, but pasta is popular nevertheless, and it is often eaten as a first course, *primo piatto*, as an alternative to soup or risotto. One type of pasta, pappardelle, is particular to this region. It is a wide ribbon noodle with pretty frilly edges, traditionally served with a sauce made of hare. Tagliatelle is another Tuscan favorite, and it can always be used in recipes calling for pappardelle. Sauces are heady, with strong-flavored ingredients. Meat, game, sausage, and offal feature prominently, especially in combination with tomatoes, onions, and garlic—and the local robust red wine.

Tagliatelle with Borlotti Beans
Tagliatelle Gustose con Fagioli

3 tablespoons olive oil

3 oz. smoked slab bacon, cubed

1 onion, finely chopped

5 sage leaves

8 oz. canned borlotti beans

¼ teaspoon flour

1 tablespoon tomato purée

2 tablespoons hot stock

2 tablespoons red wine

13 oz. tagliatelle

2 tablespoons grated Parmesan
    cheese

1 tablespoon grated Romano
    cheese

salt and pepper

4 sage sprigs, to garnish

1 Heat the oil in a large heavy pan; add the bacon, onion, and whole sage leaves. Cook over medium heat until golden. Drain the borlotti beans, rinse and drain again, then add to the pan.
2 Mix the flour and tomato purée in a small bowl; stir in the stock and wine. Pour into the bean mixture, stir with a wooden spoon, and simmer over low heat until the sauce thickens. Meanwhile, cook the pasta in plenty of salted boiling water until *al dente*, approximately 4 minutes for fresh pasta or 8 minutes for dried pasta.
3 Remove the sage leaves from the sauce, and taste and adjust the seasoning, if necessary. Drain the pasta, mix with the sauce and put in a large, heated serving dish. Add the Parmesan and Romano cheeses and serve hot, garnished with sage.

Serves 4
Preparation time: 10 minutes
Cooking time: 20 minutes

Tagliatelle with Fava Bean Sauce
Tagliatelle con Sugo di Fave

5 tablespoons butter

4 scallions, chopped

1½ lb. shelled fava beans

1 cup warm water

12 oz. tagliatelle

2 oz. smoked bacon, thinly sliced

2½ oz. Romano cheese, crumbled

1 tablespoon finely chopped
    parsley

salt and pepper

1 Heat half the butter in a pan and cook the scallions for 3 minutes.
2 Add the fava beans, allow to flavor for a few minutes, then add the warm water and continue to cook for 25 minutes. Season well.
3 Bring a pan of salted water to a boil. When the fava beans are cooked, place the pasta in the boiling water and cook until *al dente*; see recipe above. Meanwhile, fry the bacon until crisp. Drain the pasta, and dress with the remaining butter, Romano, and parsley.
4 Serve the tagliatelle topped with the bean sauce and bacon pieces.

Serves 4
Preparation time: 5 minutes
Cooking time: 45 minutes

Egg Tagliatelle
Tagliatelle all'Uovo

1¾ cups bread flour

1 teaspoon salt

3 eggs

1 tablespoon olive oil

Tagliatelle is the easiest form of homemade pasta. It can be used in recipes calling for pappardelle.

1 Sift the flour and salt into a mound on a work surface. Make a well in the center of the flour and break the eggs into the middle. Add the oil, mix with a fork, and knead the dough with your hands for about 10 minutes until it is perfectly smooth and elastic. Roll the pasta out with a rolling pin, or a pasta maker, until it is very thin.
2 Leave the pasta to dry, sprinkle with flour, then gently roll up the sheet of pasta. With a sharp knife, cut into thin strips, then shake the strips to loosen the tagliatelle. Sprinkle with flour and shake again. Cook for 4 minutes in salted boiling water.

Serves 4–6
Preparation time: 30 minutes, plus drying

Green Tagliatelle
Tagliatelle Verde

2 oz. spinach (see Cook's Notes)

1¾ cups bread flour

1 teaspoon salt

3 eggs

1 tablespoon olive oil

1 Gently heat the spinach over low heat for a few minutes, then squeeze out all the moisture by pressing in a strainer or colander with the back of a spoon. If possible, purée in a vegetable mill, blender, or food processor.
2 Prepare the dough as for tagliatelle (see above), adding the eggs and oil together with the spinach, and continue as instructed.

Cook's Notes
Frozen spinach can be used for this recipe, although it is not as tasty as fresh spinach. Defrost it first, then remove all the excess water by tossing the spinach in a pan over medium heat until it is dry.

Serves 4–6
Preparation time: 30 minutes, plus drying

Macaroni with Tomato & Rosemary
Maccheroni al Pomodoro e Rosmarino

1 Heat the oil in a heavy pan with half the butter; add the bacon, garlic, and rosemary, and cook over medium heat until golden. Add the ground beef, mix to separate the pieces, and brown; then reduce the heat. Season with salt and pepper. Drain the tomatoes and add to the pan.

2 When the sauce has reduced, pour in the stock and add the wine. Simmer until the sauce has reduced by half. Cover with a lid and simmer very gently for another 40 minutes, adding hot water if the sauce dries out.

3 Cook the macaroni in plenty of salted boiling water until *al dente;* about 4 minutes for fresh pasta or 8 minutes for dried. Drain the pasta, put it in a heated serving bowl and add the prepared sauce, remaining butter, and the Parmesan. Mix well and serve at once.

Serves 4
Preparation time: 10 minutes
Cooking time: 1 hour

3 tablespoons olive oil

4 tablespoons butter, diced

2 oz. bacon, finely chopped

2 garlic cloves, finely chopped

2 sprigs of rosemary, finely chopped

½ lb. ground beef

1¾ lb. canned plum tomatoes

1 cup beef stock

¼ cup red wine

12 oz. macaroni

1 oz. Parmesan cheese, grated

salt and pepper

Penne with Sausages & Mixed Vegetables
Penne Una Tira l'Altra

3 tablespoons olive oil

2 tablespoons butter

½ onion, finely chopped

I small shallot, finely chopped

I small carrot, finely diced

I celery stalk, sliced

¼ lb. Italian sausage, crumbled

I small yellow pepper, deseeded and diced

4 basil leaves, finely chopped

¼ cup dry red wine

14 oz. can plum tomatoes

14 oz. penne

2 tablespoons grated Romano cheese

2 tablespoons grated Parmesan cheese

salt and pepper

basil sprigs, to garnish (optional)

1 Heat the oil and butter in a flameproof casserole dish, add the onion, shallot, carrot, and celery, and cook over low heat for 4 minutes.

2 Mix well and then add the crumbled sausage, diced pepper, and chopped basil. Brown over medium heat for 3–4 minutes, then add the red wine.

3 When the wine has evaporated, strain the juice from the plum tomatoes and add them to the casserole dish with salt and pepper to taste. Cook the sauce for 30 minutes, stirring from time to time.

4 Cook the pasta in plenty of salted boiling water until *al dente*, about 4 minutes for fresh and 8 minutes for dried pasta; then drain well. Pour the pasta into the casserole and mix well. Sprinkle with the grated cheeses and mix again before serving hot. Garnish with basil sprigs, if desired.

Serves 4
Preparation time: 15 minutes
Cooking time: 50 minutes–1 hour

"The task of the Tuscan cook is not easy. He cannot fall back on elaborate sauces and gravies to disguise the flavor of the food, nor may he employ garnishes which are so dear to some schools of cooking. In preparing dishes of classic simplicity, he must rely on his skill alone, aided by the excellence of his raw materials."

Ada Boni
Italian Regional Cooking

Deep-fried Pasta
Crescentine

½ teaspoon active dry yeast

¼ teaspoon sugar

4 cups bread flour

sea salt and pepper

2 tablespoons butter, softened

½ cup lukewarm vegetable stock

vegetable oil, for deep-frying

1 Dissolve the yeast and sugar in a little warm water and set aside for 10 minutes. Sift the flour and a little salt onto a work surface. Stir in the yeast, then add the butter and just enough stock to make a soft dough. Knead well, then roll out into a fairly thick sheet.
2 Fold the 4 corners of the dough inward to the center, then flatten with the rolling pin. Fold and flatten again at least 5 times. Roll out to a sheet about ¼ inch thick, and cut into small rectangles. Deep-fry the shapes, a few at a time, in hot oil until golden and puffed up. Sprinkle with salt and pepper.

Serves 6
Preparation time: 20 minutes
Cooking time: 10 minutes

Pappardelle with Seafood Sauce
Pappardelle alla Marinara

2 lb. clams, scrubbed

5 tablespoons olive oil

½ lb. sole fillets

½ lb. cod fillet, skinned and cut into bite-sized pieces

2 onions, finely chopped

½ lb. plum tomatoes, halved and deseeded

½ lb. peeled shrimps

1 bunch of chives, chopped

12 oz. fresh pappardelle or fettuccine

salt and pepper

1 Put the clams in a large shallow pan with 1 tablespoon of the oil. Cover and cook over high heat for 5–8 minutes until open. Discard any that do not open. Remove the clams from their shells and put them in a bowl. Strain the cooking liquid through cheesecloth.
2 Heat the remaining oil in a large pan, add the onions, and salt and pepper. Cook over medium heat until golden. Add the strained clam cooking liquid and simmer for 10 minutes, then add the clams and tomatoes. Cook for 10 minutes more. Add the shrimps, followed a few minutes later by the fish pieces, and simmer for 15 minutes, until they are cooked through. Sprinkle with chives and keep hot.
3 Cook the pasta in plenty of salted boiling water for 4 minutes or until *al dente*. Drain, mix with the sauce, and serve.

Serves 4–6
Preparation time: 10 minutes
Cooking time: 50 minutes

Pasta with Seafood & Mushroom Sauce
Tagliolini Mare e Monti

PASTA:

4 cups bread flour

4 eggs

pinch of salt

1 tablespoon olive oil

SEAFOOD SAUCE:

3 tablespoons butter

1 garlic clove, crushed

12 oz. mushrooms, thinly sliced

1 lb. squid or baby octopus

½ cup dry white wine

2 lb. mussels

2 ripe tomatoes, skinned and chopped

1 lb. cooked peeled shrimps

1 tablespoon chopped parsley

salt and pepper

1 First make the pasta. Sift the flour onto a large work surface and break the eggs into the center with a generous pinch of salt. Add the oil and work into a smooth firm dough. Roll out the dough, taking care not to make it too thin. Leave to rest and dry out for a while. Roll the sheet up and cut it into thin strips with a large, sharp knife. Spread the strips out on a work surface or pastry board and sprinkle with a little flour to prevent them from sticking together.

2 To make the sauce, melt the butter in a heavy pan over low heat. Add the garlic and cook until soft but not browned. Add the sliced mushrooms to the pan and fry gently until softened.

3 Prepare the squid by cutting off the tentacles close to the head. Slit open the body bag and pull out the head, intestines, and clear spine. Wash the bag and tentacles well under cold running water and chop finely. Add to the pan along with the wine; cover and cook very gently for about 40 minutes.

4 Meanwhile, put the mussels in a large bowl, cover them with cold water and discard any that are open, cracked, or rise to the top. Scrub them well under cold running water to remove any barnacles and the beards. Boil 4 cups of water in a pan and add the mussels. Cover and bring back to a boil. Shake the pan occasionally, until the mussels open. Drain the mussels, discarding any that have not opened. Remove the mussels from their shells with a sharp knife.

5 Add the tomatoes to the mushroom mixture. Season with salt and pepper and cook for another 15 minutes, then add the shelled mussels, shrimps, and chopped parsley. Stir together for a few minutes and keep warm.

6 Cook the pasta in plenty of salted boiling water for about 4 minutes until *al dente*. Drain well and top with the sauce. Serve immediately.

Serves 6
Preparation time: 20 minutes, plus resting
Cooking time: 1¼ hours

Spaghetti with Mussels & Tomato Sauce
Spaghetti alla Marinara

1 Put the mussels in a large bowl, cover them with cold water, and discard any that are open, cracked, or rise to the top. Scrub them well under cold running water to remove any barnacles and the beards. Place in a large saucepan with ½ cup water, cover with a lid and cook over moderate heat until the mussels open, shaking the pan occasionally. Discard any mussels that do not open. Drain the mussels and remove their shells, leaving a few in their shells for the garnish.

2 Heat the olive oil in a skillet and add the onion and garlic. Sauté over medium heat until golden, but not brown. Add the chopped tomatoes and season with salt and pepper. Cook gently over low heat until the mixture is thickened and reduced.

3 Add the shelled mussels and mix gently into the tomato sauce. Simmer the mixture over low heat for 2–3 minutes, or until the mussels are heated through.

4 Meanwhile, cook the pasta in plenty of salted boiling water until *al dente*, about 4 minutes for fresh or 8 minutes for dried. Drain well and gently toss with the tomato and mussel sauce. Transfer to a serving dish or 4 warm plates, sprinkle with chopped parsley, and garnish with the reserved mussels.

Serves 4
Preparation time: 15 minutes
Cooking time: 25 minutes

4 pints mussels

3 tablespoons olive oil

I onion, chopped

3 garlic cloves, crushed

1½ lb. tomatoes, skinned and chopped

I lb. spaghetti

3 tablespoons chopped parsley

salt and pepper

"The Etruscans, as everyone knows, were the people who occupied the middle of Italy in early Roman days, and whom the Romans, in their usual neighborly fashion, wiped out entirely in order to make room for Rome with a very big R."

D.H. Lawrence
Etruscan Places

Country-style Macaroni
Maccheroni alla Rustica

2 anchovy fillets, soaked in a little milk

4 tablespoons olive oil

1 whole garlic clove, whole

2 oz. smoked bacon, diced

14 oz. canned plum tomatoes

2 oz. pitted black olives, chopped

¼ teaspoon chopped oregano

12 oz. macaroni

1 oz. Romano cheese, grated

salt and pepper

1 Drain the anchovies. Heat the oil in a small pan; add the garlic and anchovies. Cook over medium heat for a few minutes, then remove the garlic and add the bacon. Add the tomatoes to the pan when the bacon is crisp. Season with salt and pepper and cook on low heat for about 20 minutes until the sauce thickens. Add the olives and oregano halfway through the cooking time.

2 Cook the pasta in plenty of salted boiling water until *al dente*. Drain, transfer to a heated serving dish, pour on the sauce and sprinkle with Romano.

Serves 4
Preparation time: 10 minutes
Cooking time: 40 minutes

Pappardelle with Hare
Pappardelle con la Lepre

1 prepared hare or rabbit, cut into small pieces

2 cups red wine

1 celery stalk, chopped

1 onion, finely sliced

1 bay leaf

a few black peppercorns

3 oz. pork belly

1 carrot, roughly chopped

4 tablespoons olive oil

7 tablespoons beef stock

13 oz. pappardelle

3 oz. Parmesan cheese, grated

¼ cup butter, softened

salt and pepper

1 Put the hare, wine, celery, half the onion, the bay leaf, and peppercorns in a bowl. Marinate for 3–4 hours, stirring occasionally.

2 Grind the pork with the remaining onion and the carrot. Heat the oil in a pan, add the ground mixture, and fry for 5 minutes.

3 Drain the hare, reserving the marinade; then add to the pan with salt and pepper to taste. Fry until browned on all sides, then add 2–3 tablespoons of the reserved marinade and the stock. Cover and cook for 1½ hours until the hare is tender, stirring occasionally and adding more marinade and stock as necessary. Transfer the pieces of hare to a warmed serving dish. Strain the cooking juices and keep hot.

4 Cook the pappardelle in salted boiling water until *al dente*, about 4 minutes for fresh or 8 for dried, then drain. Pile on a serving dish and moisten with a little cooking liquor from the hare. Add the Parmesan and butter and mix. Serve with the hare in a separate dish.

Serves 4
Preparation time: 15 minutes, plus marinating
Cooking time: 1¾ hours

Penne with Black Olives
Penne alle Olive Nere

14 oz. penne

2 tablespoons olive oil

¼ cup butter, diced

I small onion, finely chopped

I celery stalk, finely chopped

I red pepper, deseeded and finely chopped

2 tablespoons dry white wine

2 tablespoons black olive purée

2 oz. pitted black olives, chopped

6 tablespoons light cream

2 tablespoons Gruyère cheese

salt and pepper

1 Cook the pasta in plenty of salted boiling water until *al dente*, about 4 minutes for fresh or 8 minutes for dried.
2 Meanwhile, heat the oil with half the butter in a large pan; add the chopped vegetables and cook over medium heat until golden.
3 Add the wine, simmer until it evaporates, then mix in the olive purée, the black olives, and the cream.
4 Drain the pasta and return it to the pan with the sauce. Add the Gruyère and remaining butter and mix. Season, leave on low heat, pour into a large serving dish.

Serves 4
Preparation time: 10 minutes
Cooking time: 20 minutes

Spaghetti with Arugula & Ricotta
Spaghetti con la Rucola e la Ricotta

10 oz. dried spaghetti

I tablespoon olive oil

2 tablespoons butter

I small onion, finely chopped

I bunch of arugula, roots trimmed and leaves finely chopped

I garlic clove, finely chopped

4 oz. ricotta cheese

½ cup dry white wine

salt and pepper

freshly grated Parmesan cheese, to serve

1 Plunge the spaghetti into a large saucepan of salted boiling water and simmer for 10–12 minutes or until *al dente*.
2 Meanwhile, heat the oil and butter in a pan until foaming. Add the onion and cook gently, stirring for 5 minutes until softened.
3 Add the arugula, garlic, and salt and pepper to taste, and stir for 2–3 minutes until wilted. Add the ricotta and wine and stir until the ricotta has melted and mixed evenly with the arugula.
4 Drain the spaghetti, return to the pan and add the arugula mixture. Toss well to combine. Serve sprinkled with Parmesan.

Cook's Notes
Spinach can be used instead of arugula, but be generous with the pepper.

Serves 4
Preparation time: 10 minutes
Cooking time: 12 minutes

Gnocchi with Pesto
Gnocchi al Pesto

A dish from the far north of Tuscany near the border with Liguria, where pesto originated.

1 First make the pesto sauce: put the basil and pine nuts into a mortar with the garlic, and season with salt and pepper. Pound together until reduced to a thick paste. Transfer to a bowl; add the oil, a little at a time, stirring constantly until thick. Stir in the lemon juice and Parmesan cheese; cover and set aside.

2 Make the gnocchi: drain the potatoes well and shake over the heat to dry them thoroughly. Mash them very finely so there are no lumps. Beat in the flour and egg and season with nutmeg and salt and pepper. Mix to a dough and turn out onto a floured board.

3 With floured hands, roll small pieces of dough into croquettes, about the thickness of your thumb. Press them lightly with the prongs of a fork—this will help them to hold the pesto.

4 Bring some lightly salted water to a boil in a large pan. Drop the gnocchi, a few at a time, into the boiling water and cook for 3–5 minutes. They will rise to the surface and float when they are cooked. Remove and drain. Arrange the gnocchi in a buttered serving dish, dot with butter and sprinkle with Parmesan cheese. Pour the pesto sauce over the top and serve immediately.

Serves 4
Preparation time: 25 minutes
Cooking time: 15 minutes

GNOCCHI:
1 lb. potatoes, freshly boiled
1¼ cups flour
1 egg, beaten
grated nutmeg
salt and pepper

PESTO SAUCE:
2 oz. fresh basil leaves, roughly chopped
1 oz. pine nuts, roughly chopped
2 garlic cloves
4 tablespoons olive oil
juice of ½ lemon
1½ oz. grated Parmesan cheese

TO SERVE:
3 tablespoons butter
grated Parmesan cheese

Pappardelle with Chicken Liver Ragù
Pappardelle con il Ragù di Fegatini

2 tablespoons olive oil

¼ lb. pancetta, diced small

1 onion, finely chopped

½ lb. ground beef

2 cups hot beef stock

14 oz. can chopped Italian plum tomatoes

½ cup red or white wine

1 tablespoon tomato purée

1 garlic clove, crushed

1 teaspoon dried sage

¼ lb. frozen chicken livers, defrosted and diced

10 oz. fresh pappardelle (see Cook's Notes)

salt and pepper

freshly grated Parmesan cheese, to serve

A Tuscan meat ragù often includes chicken livers, which enrich the sauce and give it body.

1 Heat the oil in a heavy saucepan; add the diced pancetta and chopped onion and cook, stirring, over low to medium heat until the pancetta starts to crisp.

2 Add the ground beef and cook for a few minutes until it changes color, stirring and pressing it constantly to break up any lumps.

3 Add half of the hot stock, then the tomatoes, wine, tomato purée, garlic, sage and salt and pepper to taste. Bring to a boil, then lower the heat, half cover and simmer gently for 30 minutes, stirring the pan occasionally.

4 Add the chicken livers and the remaining hot stock. Stir well to mix, then continue cooking as before for another 30 minutes.

5 Toward the end of cooking, plunge the pasta into a large saucepan of salted boiling water and simmer for 2–3 minutes or until *al dente*. Drain thoroughly, then place in a large serving bowl.

6 Taste and adjust the seasoning of the sauce, if necessary, then pour the sauce over the pasta and toss quickly to mix. Serve immediately, sprinkled with grated Parmesan cheese.

Cook's Notes
Pappardelle are wide noodles with frilly edges. They are made fresh in Tuscany, and are traditionally served with a thick hare or wild boar sauce. You can make fresh egg pasta yourself at home (see page 50), and cut ribbons almost ½ inch wide to make your own pappardelle. If you use a fluted pasta wheel for cutting, this will make the edges frilly. Alternatively, you can serve the ragù with dried noodles such as tagliatelle, or with any other pasta shape you like.

Serves 6–8
Preparation time: 20 minutes
Cooking time: 1 hour

fish

Along the coast of the Ligurian Sea, fish and shellfish are the order of the day, and there is a huge variety to choose from. Many fish are unique to these waters, and these are often to be found in the local fish stews and soups, the most famous of which is *cacciucco*, from Livorno—a kind of Tuscan equivalent of the French *bouillabaisse*. Squid, octopus, and eel are simmered in wine, and are sometimes hot with chilies, while mollusks are steamed open with garlic and fragrant herbs. Simplicity is the keynote for most seafood, and charbroiling over coals or wood is the favorite cooking method for freshly caught mullet, tuna, shark, and similar fish.

Shark with Tomatoes & Chilies
Palombo alla Livornese

4 tablespoons olive oil

3 garlic cloves, crushed

2 fresh red chilies, deseeded and finely chopped

1 lb. ripe plum tomatoes, roughly chopped

1 glass of red wine, preferably Chianti

1 teaspoon chopped fresh sage

4 shark steaks

salt and pepper

finely chopped flat-leaf parsley, to garnish

The term "alla Livornese" is used to describe fish and shellfish from the coastal town of Livorno, often cooked in a tomato sauce. Palombo—shark—is fished off this coast, and its firm, meaty flesh holds its own against the robust flavor of the tomato sauce.

1 Heat the oil in a large flameproof casserole; add the garlic and chilies and cook very gently, stirring constantly, for about 5 minutes until softened.

2 Add the tomatoes, wine, sage, and salt and pepper to taste, and bring to a boil. Cover and simmer very gently, stirring occasionally, for 30 minutes.

3 Add the shark steaks to the sauce, cover and cook gently for 10-15 minutes until tender when pierced with a fork. Taste the sauce for seasoning, and adjust if necessary. Serve hot, sprinkled with chopped parsley.

Cook's Notes

Tuna and swordfish are also good cooked this way because they are strong, meaty fish, like shark. Chunks of monkfish fillets can also be used because they are firm in texture and hold their shape well. All of these fish can be found at large supermarkets, but their seasons vary, so you may not be able to get the fresh fish when you want it. Frozen fish is very good, but be sure to defrost it properly first, then pat it thoroughly dry with paper towels before you start cooking.

Chili powder can be used instead of fresh chilies, but be cautious with the brand, because some are very hot and fiery. For this dish, 1 teaspoon mild chili powder is sufficient not to overpower the flavor of the fish.

Serves 4
Preparation time: 5 minutes
Cooking time: 40–45 minutes

Monkfish with Tomatoes & Garlic
Pesce alla Pizzaiola

4 x 5 oz. monkfish steaks

3 tablespoons olive oil

MARINADE:

5 tablespoons olive oil

juice of ½ lemon

1 tablespoon finely chopped fresh
 parsley

TOMATO SAUCE:

2 tablespoons olive oil

4 garlic cloves, chopped

1½ lb. tomatoes, skinned
 and chopped

4 anchovy fillets, chopped

salt and pepper

1 tablespoon chopped oregano, to
 garnish

1 Wash the monkfish steaks under cold running water and pat dry with paper towels. Put all the marinade ingredients in a bowl and mix well together.

2 Add the monkfish steaks to the marinade, turning them until they are thoroughly coated and glistening with oil. Cover the bowl and leave in a cool place to marinate for at least 1 hour.

3 Heat the olive oil in a large skillet. Remove the fish steaks from the marinade and fry gently until they are cooked and golden brown on both sides, turning the fish once during cooking. Remove the steaks from the pan and keep them warm.

4 While the fish steaks are cooking, make the tomato sauce. Heat the olive oil in a pan and sauté the garlic until just golden. Add the tomatoes and chopped anchovies and cook over medium heat until the tomatoes are reduced to a thick pulpy consistency. Season to taste with salt and pepper. Pour the sauce over the fish and sprinkle with oregano, to garnish.

Serves 4
Preparation time: 10–15 minutes, plus marinating
Cooking time: 20 minutes

Sea Bass in Sweet & Sour Sauce
Spigola in Agrodolce

Spigola—sea bass—is very popular in coastal resorts, and highly prized for its soft flesh and delicate flavor. When freshly caught, it is best cooked as simply as possible, preferably grilled over coals and served with nothing more than a sprinkling of olive oil and a squeeze of lemon. This recipe, with its strong flavors of wine vinegar, sugar, and raisins, is best suited to the sea bass you will buy at the grocery store.

1 Season the flour with salt and pepper. Cut the fish fillets on the diagonal into serving pieces, then coat in the seasoned flour.
2 Heat the oil and butter together in a large non-stick skillet until foaming.
3 Add as many pieces of fish as the pan will hold and fry over medium heat for 1–2 minutes on each side, until crisp and golden. Remove the fish pieces with a slotted spoon and set aside on a plate. Repeat with any remaining pieces of fish if necessary.
4 Add the remaining ingredients to the pan with salt and pepper to taste, and stir over moderate to high heat until reduced.
5 Return the fish to the pan, then shake the pan and spoon the sauce over until the pieces are evenly coated. Serve immediately.

Cook's Notes
Sea bass is an expensive fish, and size varies according to season, so check with your supplier for the best time to buy it. Other white fish fillets can be used if you prefer. Sole is also traditional with a sweet and sour sauce in Italian cooking, but you can use plaice, or even cod or haddock fillets.

Serves 4
Preparation time: 10 minutes
Cooking time: about 10 minutes

1½ tablespoons flour

4 sea bass fillets

2 tablespoons olive oil

1 tablespoon butter

1 cup dry white wine

2 tablespoons white wine vinegar

1 tablespoon sugar

2 tablespoons raisins

salt and pepper

Tuna Livorno Style
Tonno alla Livornese

4 fresh tuna steaks

½ cup flour

4 tablespoons olive oil

I small onion, finely chopped

4 sprigs of parsley, finely chopped

½ cup dry white wine

I tablespoon capers, drained

I bay leaf, crumbled

¼ teaspoon ground cinnamon

salt and pepper

1 Coat the tuna steaks in flour. Heat the oil in a heavy pan, mix the onion and parsley together, and add them to the pan. Sauté over medium heat, stirring, until just golden, but not brown.
2 Add the tuna steaks and cook for 2 minutes on each side. Season with salt and pepper and pour over the wine. Leave until this has evaporated a little, then add the capers, crumbled bay leaf, and cinnamon. Cover and cook for 15 minutes, adding water if needed.
3 Serve the tuna steaks with the cooking juices poured over, accompanied with new potatoes and a green salad.

Serves 4
Preparation time: 5 minutes
Cooking time: 25 minutes

Mackerel with Olives & Tomatoes
Sgombri alle Olive e Pomodoro

4 x 12 oz. mackerel

2 tablespoons flour

4 tablespoons olive oil

I garlic clove, crushed

3 anchovy fillets

8 oz. canned plum tomatoes, drained and chopped

24 pitted black olives, halved

½ cup fish stock

I tablespoon chopped parsley

salt and pepper

1 Clean, dry, and lightly flour the mackerel. Heat the oil in a large pan, add the crushed garlic and anchovies, and cook over medium heat until the garlic is lightly browned. Add the fish and cook for a few minutes, turning once.
2 Add the tomatoes along with the olives. Continue to cook, adding fish stock from time to time, for about 30 minutes, until the fish is cooked and the sauce well thickened. Season to taste and sprinkle with parsley just before the end of the cooking time.
3 Serve the fish with the sauce poured over. This is delicious served with a country bread.

Serves 4
Preparation time: 10 minutes
Cooking time: 35–40 minutes

Gray Mullet in Garlic Breadcrumbs
Pesce all'Aglio

2 lbs. gray mullet fillets

1 egg

3 garlic cloves

1 sprig of rosemary

4 tablespoons dried breadcrumbs

peanut oil, for frying

salt and pepper

1 lemon, cut into wedges, to serve

Although this dish is traditionally made with gray mullet, any flaky-fleshed white fish, such as sea bass, red mullet, or even cod can be used instead.

1 Wash the fillets under cold running water, drain, dry, and flatten out. Beat the egg with 3–4 tablespoons water on a flat plate.
2 Finely chop the garlic with the rosemary. Add to the breadcrumbs and season with salt and pepper. Coat the fish first in egg and then in the breadcrumb mixture, making sure it sticks well.
3 Heat the oil in a large shallow pan over medium heat. Add the fish and fry, turning once, until cooked through and golden; about 8 minutes total.
4 Drain on paper towels and arrange on a heated plate. Serve accompanied with wedges of lemon.

Serves 4
Preparation time: 10–15 minutes
Cooking time: 30 minutes

"...fair Italy!
Thou art the garden of the world, the home
Of all art yields, and nature can decree;
Even in thy desert, what is like to thee?
Thy very weeds are beautiful—thy waste
More rich than other climes fertility;
Thy wreck a glory, and thy ruin graced
With an immaculate charm which cannot be defaced."

Lord Byron
Childe Harold's Pilgrimage

Red Mullet Baked in Foil
Triglie al Cartoccio

1 Clean and dry the fish and season with salt and pepper.
2 Grease a large sheet of foil with some of the butter. Put half the tomatoes in the center along with half the capers. Sprinkle with half the basil, half the remaining diced butter, and half the olives. Put the fish on top and cover with the remaining ingredients.
3 Close the foil tightly, put on a cookie sheet and bake in a preheated oven at 400°F for 35 minutes.
4 Transfer to a serving dish, open the foil slightly, and serve.

Serves 4
Preparation time: 5 minutes
Cooking time: 35 minutes

4 red mullet

4 tablespoons butter, diced

8 oz. canned plum tomatoes, drained

1 tablespoon capers, drained

1 tablespoon roughly chopped basil

16 pitted black olives, chopped

salt and pepper

Sole with Parmesan
Sogliole alla Parmigiana

1 Skin the sole. Put some flour in a shallow bowl and season with salt and pepper. Dip the sole into the seasoned flour to dust them lightly on both sides. Shake off any excess flour.
2 Heat the butter in a large skillet. Add the floured sole and cook over gentle heat until they are golden brown on both sides, turning them once during cooking.
3 Sprinkle the grated Parmesan over the sole, and then cook very gently for another 2–3 minutes until the cheese melts.
4 Add the fish stock and the Marsala or white wine. Cover the pan and cook over very low heat for 4–5 minutes, until the sole are cooked and tender and the sauce reduced. Serve sprinkled with grated Parmesan and accompany with lemon wedges.

Serves 4
Preparation time: 5 minutes
Cooking time: 15–20 minutes

4 lemon sole

flour, for dusting

6 tablespoons butter

1 oz. Parmesan cheese, grated

¼ cup fish stock

3 tablespoons Marsala or white wine

salt and pepper

TO SERVE:

grated Parmesan cheese

lemon wedges

Sole Florentine

Filetti di Sogliola Gratinati alla Fiorentina

14 oz. fresh spinach

2 tablespoons butter

4 sole fillets, skinned

2 teaspoons olive oil

½ cup dry white wine

½ cup fish stock

Parmesan cheese, grated

salt and pepper

WHITE SAUCE:

4 tablespoons butter

1½ cups milk

½ cup flour

¼ teaspoon grated nutmeg

2–3 tablespoons light cream

2 oz. Gruyère cheese, grated

salt and pepper

1 Wash the spinach thoroughly, removing any coarse stems. Drain, then cook in a deep pan for 5 minutes in just the water remaining on the leaves. Drain and mix with the butter.

2 Put the sole fillets into an oiled flameproof dish, cover with the wine and fish stock; season with salt and pepper. Bake in a preheated oven, 350°F (180°C), for 15 minutes.

3 Remove the fish and keep hot. Put the dish over high heat to reduce the cooking juices to about 2–3 tablespoons.

4 Next prepare the white sauce: melt the butter in a small pan and heat the milk in a separate pan. Stir the flour into the butter, then add the hot milk gradually, stirring vigorously to ensure that no lumps form. Season with salt, pepper, and nutmeg, and stir well over low heat until thick and cooked.

5 Add the reduced fish juices and cream; cook for another 5 minutes to reduce the sauce a little more, then add the Gruyère.

6 Brush an ovenproof serving dish with oil and arrange the spinach on the bottom of the dish. Put the sole fillets on top; cover with the white sauce and top with Parmesan. Put in a preheated oven, 400°F (200°C), for approximately 10 minutes until the top is crisp and golden. Serve hot.

Serves 4
Preparation time: 30 minutes
Cooking time: 25 minutes

Squid Braised with Red Wine & Garlic
Calamari dei Pescatore

This simple dish cooks by itself in the oven, so there is little for you to do, especially if you buy ready-prepared squid from the supermarket. To soak up the delicious juices, serve it with boiled rice or polenta (see Polenta with Wild Boar on page 80).

1 Put the squid, onion, and garlic in an ovenproof dish with salt and pepper to taste. Pour in the wine and wine vinegar and add enough water to cover the squid.

2 Cover the dish and place in a preheated oven, 350°F, for 45 minutes or until tender. The best way to test for tenderness is to remove a piece of squid from the liquid and bite into it.

3 Serve the squid straight from the dish, sprinkled with parsley.

Cook's Notes

A suitable Tuscan wine to use for this dish is Chianti. If you buy a good-quality Chianti Classico, from the area between Florence and Siena, you can enjoy drinking the rest of the bottle with the meal.

If you like, you can add a few sliced wild or cultivated mushrooms to the squid for the last 15 minutes of cooking.

The squid can be prepared up to 24 hours in advance and reheated.

Serves 4
Preparation time: 5 minutes
Cooking time: 45 minutes

1 lb. prepared squid rings

1 red onion, sliced thinly into rings

2 garlic cloves, finely chopped

1 cup full-bodied red wine
(see Cook's Notes)

2 tablespoons red wine vinegar

salt and pepper

finely chopped flat-leaf parsley, to garnish

Cod with Vegetables
Merluzzo con Verdure

½ teaspoon saffron strands

1¼ lb. cod fillet

1 tablespoon flour

3 tablespoons olive oil

2 yellow peppers, deseeded and
 sliced into slivers

2 tomatoes, quartered

1 small onion, finely chopped

1 garlic clove, finely chopped

1 tablespoon chopped parsley

salt and pepper

slices of polenta, to serve (see
 Cook's Notes)

1 Soak the saffron strands in a little hot water. Cut the cod into even-sized pieces and dust with flour. Heat the oil in a large shallow pan; add the cod and cook over medium heat for a few minutes, turning once, until golden. Season with salt and pepper, remove with a spatula and keep warm.

2 Add the peppers, tomatoes, onion, and garlic to the pan and sauté until golden. Season with a pinch of salt, reduce the heat, cover with a lid and simmer for about 30 minutes. Stir in the saffron liquid halfway through.

3 When the vegetables are almost cooked, add the pieces of cod and sprinkle with chopped parsley. Serve hot, accompanied by slices of polenta (see Cook's Notes).

Cook's Notes
This dish tastes particularly good accompanied by slices of grilled polenta. Quick-cooking polenta can be bought at Italian delicatessens and some supermarkets. It is very easy to prepare. Its attractive yellow color gives the cod an extra lift.

Serves 4
Preparation time: 5 minutes
Cooking time: 35 minutes

"But in those days, on a fine evening like this, the men would come in naked, darkly ruddy-colored from the sun and wind, with strong, insouciant bodies; and the women would drift in, wearing the loose becoming smock of white or blue linen; and somebody, surely, would be playing on the pipes; and somebody, surely, would be singing, because the Etruscans had a passion for music, and an inner carelessness the modern Italians have lost."

D.H. Lawrence
Etruscan Places

meat,
poultry &
game

Is it any wonder that the Tuscans are such great meat eaters when they have some of the best beef in the world? The cattle in the *Val di Chiana* are renowned for their succulent, tasty meat, and no self-respecting Tuscan chef would prepare *bistecca alla Fiorentina* without it. *La Fiorentina*, as it is affectionately called, is simply charbroiled over a wood fire, a method that is adopted for many other meats and game birds in this region. The reason for this is simple—the meat is of such high quality that it needs nothing more than brief cooking and a simple sprinkling of olive oil, salt, and pepper. At the other end of the scale, older, tougher cuts are simmered slowly in rich wine sauces to produce tender, tasty morsels that literally melt in the mouth.

Polenta with Wild Boar
Polenta con Cinghiale

2 lbs. boneless wild boar, cut into large cubes

6 tablespoons olive oil

1 onion, finely chopped

1 carrot, finely chopped

1 celery stalk, finely chopped

1 garlic clove, crushed

4 Italian pork sausages (see Cook's Notes for Sausages with Beans & Sage, page 90), cut into chunks

about 2 cups beef stock

½ cup passata (tomato sauce)

2 tablespoons chopped flat-leaf parsley

2 teaspoons dried sage

1 teaspoon dried thyme

salt and pepper

MARINADE:

750 ml bottle of full-bodied red wine

1 onion, roughly chopped

1 carrot, roughly chopped

1 celery stalk, roughly chopped

1 bay leaf, torn

1 sprig each of sage and rosemary

1 tablespoon crushed black peppercorns

1 tablespoon crushed juniper berries

POLENTA:

3 cups water

1 cup milk

1 teaspoon salt

8 oz. pre-cooked polenta (see Cook's Notes)

4 tablespoons butter

fresh chopped sage leaves, to garnish

1 Start by making the marinade. Put all the ingredients for the marinade in a saucepan and bring to a boil. Pour into a bowl, leave to cool, then add the wild boar. Cover and marinate in the refrigerator overnight, or up to 2 days.

2 Remove the meat from the marinade with a slotted spoon and pat dry with paper towels. Strain the marinade into a container.

3 Heat 4 tablespoons of the oil in a flameproof casserole; add the onion, carrot, celery, and garlic and cook gently, stirring frequently, for about 5 minutes until softened.

4 Add about one-quarter of the marinated meat and cook over medium to high heat, stirring frequently, until browned on all sides. Remove with a slotted spoon and set aside on a plate. Repeat with the remaining meat and the sausages, adding more oil as necessary.

5 Add the strained marinade, the stock, and passata, and bring to a boil. Lower the heat and add the herbs, and season with salt and pepper to taste. Cover and cook in a preheated oven, 325°F, for 2 hours or until the meat is tender.

6 Cook the polenta: bring the water and milk to a boil in a large pan, add the salt, then sprinkle in the polenta in a thin, steady stream, stirring all the time. Cook over medium heat, stirring constantly, for 8 minutes or according to the package instructions. Remove from the heat and beat in the butter until melted.

7 To serve: taste the stew and the polenta for seasoning. Divide the polenta between 6 plates, then spoon the stew around. Garnish with chopped sage.

Cook's Notes

You can substitute venison for wild boar. The flavor of this dish benefits from being served the day after making. Leave to cool and refrigerate, then reheat thoroughly 24 hours later.

Polenta has to be stirred continuously during cooking or it will be lumpy. Be sure to buy the instant or quick-cooking type of polenta from an Italian delicatessen or large supermarket—otherwise you will find it to be hard work. The polenta spits and sputters during cooking, so be careful while standing over the pan, and use a long-handled spoon.

Serves 6
Preparation time: 30 minutes, plus marinating
Cooking time: 2 hours

Beef Braised in Red Wine

Brasato al Barolo

3 lbs. beef; eye of the round or rolled flank steak or chuck roast

2 tablespoons bacon fat or drippings

1 onion, finely chopped

1 sprig of rosemary

salt and pepper

MARINADE:

1 onion, sliced

1 carrot, sliced

1 celery stalk, sliced

2 garlic cloves, crushed

2 bay leaves

6 peppercorns

2 cups Barolo or other red wine

1 First marinate the beef. Put the meat in a deep bowl and add the onion, carrot, celery, garlic, bay leaves, peppercorns, and the red wine. Cover the bowl and place in the refrigerator to marinate for 24 hours, turning the beef several times. Lift the meat out of the marinade and dry it carefully. Reserve the marinade.

2 Heat the bacon fat or drippings in a large flameproof casserole and sauté the chopped onion over low heat for about 5 minutes, or until it is soft and golden. Add the beef, increase the heat, and brown quickly on all sides.

3 Strain the reserved marinade into the casserole and bring to a boil. Add the rosemary and season with salt and pepper. Lower the heat, cover tightly and simmer gently for at least 3 hours, or until the meat is tender. Turn the meat once halfway through cooking.

4 Transfer the meat to a carving dish or board and slice fairly thickly. Arrange the slices on a warm serving dish. If the sauce is too thin, reduce a little by rapid boiling. Remove the rosemary and pour the sauce over the meat. Serve immediately, with puréed potatoes and carrots.

Serves 6
Preparation time: 10 minutes, plus marinating
Cooking time: 3–3½ hours

Stuffed Beef Olives
Involtini al Sugo

1 Cut the beef into thin slices and place between 2 sheets of waxed paper. Flatten them with a rolling pin and then season with salt and pepper.

2 Next make the filling: put the grated Romano cheese in a bowl with the chopped ham, garlic, parsley, and basil. Mix well together and spread a little of this mixture onto each slice of beef. Roll up, folding in the sides, and secure with fine string.

3 Heat the olive oil in a large saucepan and gently fry the beef rolls until they are slightly brown all over, turning as necessary. Remove from the pan and keep warm.

4 Finally, make the sauce: add the onion and garlic to the oil in the pan and sauté until soft. Add the tomatoes, tomato purée, and wine, and season with salt and pepper. Bring to a boil, and then add the beef rolls. Cover and simmer gently for 1½–2 hours or until tender. Remove the string from the beef rolls and serve with the sauce, sprinkled with basil.

Serves 6
Preparation time: 10–15 minutes
Cooking time: about 2 hours

2 lbs. beef, eye of the round

4 oz. Romano cheese, grated

2 slices of raw ham (prosciutto crudo), chopped

3 garlic cloves, crushed

3 tablespoons chopped fresh parsley

1 tablespoon chopped fresh basil

3 tablespoons olive oil

salt and pepper

TOMATO SAUCE:

1 onion, chopped

2 garlic cloves, crushed

2 lbs. tomatoes, skinned and chopped

1 tablespoon tomato purée

½ cup red wine

salt and pepper

a few basil leaves, torn, to garnish

"For July, in Siena, by the willow tree,
I give you barrels of white Tuscan wine
In ice far down your cellars stored supine;"

Folgore da San Gemigano
Translated by Dante Gabriel Rossetti

Florentine Grilled Steak

La Fiorentina

1 T-bone steak, 1–1½ inches thick

about 2 tablespoons olive oil

salt and pepper

This must be Tuscany's most famous dish. It is unbelievably simple to make, but it does need good steak. A Tuscan chef will tell you that only the best Val de Chiana *beef will do, so if you are cooking on vacation in Tuscany, you can buy some and find out for yourself.*

1 Prepare the barbecue and let it burn until the flames have died down and the coals have turned gray.

2 Put the steak on the barbecue grill and cook for 5 minutes, then turn the steak over and sprinkle the cooked side with salt and pepper. Cook for another 5 minutes, turn again and sprinkle the second cooked side with salt and pepper. Cook for 2 minutes.

3 Remove the steak from the barbecue grill and sprinkle with olive oil. Serve immediately.

Cook's Notes

La Fiorentina is traditionally served very rare, and the cooking time given here is for rare steak, but you can cook the steak longer if you prefer. Another version of this dish is Florentine Steak Tagliatelle with Arugula (Tagliata alla Fiorentina con Rucola). Cook boneless rump steaks on the barbecue, then cut each steak into thin diagonal slices. Arrange the slices on individual plates and sprinkle with chopped arugula, olive oil, and salt and pepper to taste.

Serves 2

Preparation time: 1–2 minutes, plus time to prepare the barbecue
Cooking time: 12 minutes

"Nowhere in Italy are the steaks so good, so full of flavor and at the same time so tender as in Tuscany."

Elizabeth David
Italian Food

Beef Steaks with Mozzarella
Bistecche del Buon Tempo

2 tablespoons butter

4 beef steaks

2 tablespoons olive oil

1 onion, finely chopped

1 garlic clove, crushed

1 zucchini, cut into matchstick strips

1 yellow pepper, deseeded and cut into strips

1 eggplant, trimmed and diced

6 plum tomatoes, skinned and chopped

10 basil leaves, chopped

8 slices of mozzarella cheese

salt and pepper

1 Melt the butter in a shallow pan over medium heat, put in the steaks and cook for 2–4 minutes on each side or according to taste. Season, remove from the pan and keep warm.

2 Add the oil to the same pan and sauté the onion and garlic until golden, but not brown. Add the prepared vegetables and cook for a few minutes. Add the tomatoes to the pan with a little salt and pepper; sprinkle with basil.

3 Cut 4 pieces of foil large enough to wrap around the steaks with room to spare. Put a steak in the center of each and top with ¼ of the vegetables and 2 slices of Mozzarella cheese. Pinch the edges of the foil together and put in a preheated oven, 350°F, for 15 minutes to melt the cheese. Serve at once.

Serves 4
Preparation time: 15 minutes
Cooking time: 35 minutes

Steak with Olives
Filetto alle Olive

1 garlic clove, cut into small slivers

2½ lbs. fillet of beef

6 tablespoons butter

¼ cup dry white wine

1 cup beef stock

1 tablespoon flour

8 oz. green olives, pitted and finely chopped

1½ tablespoons chopped parsley

salt and pepper

1 Dust the garlic slivers with salt and pepper. Make small slits all over the meat and push the garlic slivers inside.
Melt half the butter in a flameproof casserole over medium heat. Add the meat and brown it lightly on all sides. Sprinkle on the wine and continue cooking until it has evaporated. Add the stock, cover and cook for 20 minutes. Remove the meat and keep hot.

2 Melt the remaining butter in a small pan; stir in the flour and cooking juices from the meat. Cook over low heat for 10 minutes, stirring occasionally. Add the olives to the sauce with the parsley.

3 Serve the meat sliced and covered with the sauce.

Serves 6
Preparation time: 10 minutes
Cooking time: 50 minutes

Braised Beef with Endive
Manzo Brasato all'Indivia

1 Mix the mixed spice with the rosemary, garlic, and a little pepper. Cut the bacon fat into small strips (1½ x ½ inch) and roll in the chopped mixture. Using a sharp-pointed knife, make slits in the beef and insert the strips of fat.

2 Heat the oil and butter in a large flameproof casserole, add the chopped onion, celery, and chicory, and cook over very low heat for 10 minutes. Dust the meat with flour, add to the pan, and brown lightly all over, stirring the vegetables with a wooden spoon to prevent burning. Season with a little salt, then remove the meat and put aside on a plate.

3 Add 1 tablespoon flour to the pan, stir into the cooking juices and then add the milk, crumbled bouillon cube, and half the wine. Stir until well mixed, add the meat and leave on low heat for a few minutes to blend the flavors. Add the remaining wine and the stock and cook over low heat for 50 minutes, adding a little water from time to time.

4 Remove the meat, carve and keep warm. Put the sauce in a blender or food processor with the cream and process until smooth and creamy. Reheat gently and serve with the meat.

Serves 4
Preparation time: 15 minutes
Cooking time: 1 hour

¼ teaspoon mixed spice

I large sprig of rosemary, finely chopped

I garlic clove, finely chopped

½ cup bacon fat

1½ lbs. lean beef, eye of the round

½ cup olive oil

4 tablespoons butter

I small onion, finely chopped

I celery stalk, finely chopped

2 chicory heads, finely chopped

3–4 tablespoons flour

I cup milk

I beef bouillon cube

I cup dry white wine

2 tablespoons beef stock

2 tablespoons light cream

salt and pepper

"O love, what hours were thine and mine,
In lands of palm and southern pine;
In lands of palm, of orange blossom,
Of olive, aloe, and maize and vine."

Tennyson

Countryman's Roast Beef

Arrosto di Manzo del Contadino

2 eggs

1 bunch of basil, finely chopped

1 garlic clove, finely chopped

2 tablespoons grated Parmesan cheese

4 tablespoons olive oil

2 red peppers

1½ lb. thick slice of sirloin

3 oz. bacon slices

2 tablespoons butter

1 shallot, chopped

1 beef bouillon cube

¼ cup dry white wine

½ cup beef stock

salt and pepper

1 Beat the eggs lightly, add a little salt and pepper, and stir in the chopped basil and garlic along with the Parmesan.

2 Heat half the oil in an 8 inch shallow pan over medium heat. Pour in the egg mixture, allow to set on one side, then with the help of a lid turn the omelette over and cook the other side.

3 Char the skin of the peppers under a hot broiler or in a flame. Peel, deseed, and cut into strips.

4 Spread the meat out on a work surface and sprinkle lightly with salt. Cover with slices of bacon and put the prepared omelette on top. Add the peppers, roll up tightly, and secure with string.

5 Heat the remaining oil with the butter in a flameproof casserole, add the shallot, and cook over medium heat until golden. Then add the meat roll and brown it lightly all over. Crumble the bouillon cube into the pan, season with pepper, and moisten with the wine. Continue cooking until the wine has evaporated, then add the stock.

6 Cover and cook in a preheated oven, 375°F, for 25 minutes or until the meat is tender.

7 Slice the meat roll, arrange on a heated dish, and serve with the cooking juices poured over.

Cook's Notes

This unusual dish is very rich, but absolutely delicious. Try serving it with mashed potatoes or boiled polenta to soak up all the cooking juices.

Serves 6
Preparation time: 15 minutes
Cooking time: 1 hour

Beef and Red Wine Stew
Stracotta di Manzo

This stew is typical of the kind of robust, hearty meat dishes that Tuscans love, especially in the winter months. Serve it with mashed or creamed potatoes, or boiled polenta (see Polenta with Wild Boar on page 80).

1 Heat 2 tablespoons of the oil in a large flameproof casserole. Add about ¼ of the cubes of meat and cook over medium to high heat, stirring frequently, until browned on all sides. Remove with a slotted spoon and set aside on a plate. Repeat with the remaining meat, adding more oil as necessary.

2 Heat the remaining oil in the pan. Add the chopped carrots, onion, celery, and garlic and cook gently, stirring frequently, for about 5 minutes until softened.

3 Return all of the meat and juices to the pan, stir to mix with the vegetables, then sprinkle in the flour. Cook, stirring constantly, for 1–2 minutes, then add the wine, stock, canned tomatoes and their juice, and bring to a boil. Stir to scrape up all the sediment from the bottom and sides of the pan.

4 Add the tomato purée, herbs, bay leaf, and salt and pepper to taste.

5 Cover the pan and cook for 2–2½ hours or until the meat is tender when pierced with a fork. Taste for seasoning before serving, garnished with bay leaves.

Cook's Notes

Stracotta *means "overcooked," and traditionally this stew was cooked with a large piece of meat which literally fell apart after very long, slow cooking. To achieve a similar result, make the stew the day before required. The flavor will mellow if the stew is left to become cold and then reheated before serving, and the texture of the meat will be softer.*

To save time, chop all the vegetables together in a food processor fitted with the metal blade.

The cubes of meat should be about 1½ inches square, and well marbled with fat—meat that is too lean and cut too small will dry out and be tough. The initial browning over fairly high heat is important—this gives the stew a good color and flavor at the finish.

Serves 4–6
Preparation time: 30 minutes
Cooking time: 2–2½ hours

4 tablespoons olive oil

2 lbs. braising steak, cut into even-sized cubes

2 carrots, finely chopped

I large onion, finely chopped

2 celery stalks, finely chopped

2 garlic cloves, crushed

2 tablespoons flour

I¼ cups red wine, preferably Chianti

I¼ cups hot beef stock

½ x 14 oz. can chopped Italian plum tomatoes

2 tablespoons tomato purée

2 teaspoons dried mixed herbs

I bay leaf, torn

salt and pepper

fresh bay leaves, to garnish

Sausages with Beans & Sage
Salsiccie con Fagioli all'Uccelletto

8 oz. dried cannellini beans, soaked
 in cold water overnight

5 tablespoons olive oil

1 lb. Italian pork sausages, chopped
 (see Cook's Notes)

1 cup passata (tomato sauce)

2 garlic cloves, crushed

1 sprig of fresh sage or
 2 teaspoons dried sage

salt and pepper

fresh sage leaves, to garnish

Uccelletto is the Italian for a small bird such as a thrush or lark. The Tuscan term "all'uccelletto" is used to describe this bean dish because it is flavored with sage, an herb often used when cooking small birds.

1 Drain the beans and rinse under cold running water. Put them in a large saucepan, cover with fresh cold water, and bring to a boil. Boil rapidly for 10 minutes, then lower the heat and half cover with a lid. Simmer for 1¼ hours or until the beans are tender, skimming off the scum and adding water as necessary.

2 Drain the beans and reserve the cooking liquid.

3 Heat 3 tablespoons of the oil in a flameproof casserole or heavy saucepan, add the sausages, and cook over medium heat until browned on all sides. Add the passata, garlic, sage, and salt and pepper to taste and stir well to mix. Bring to a boil, then add the beans and a few spoonfuls of the cooking liquid. Cover and simmer, stirring frequently, for 15 minutes—the consistency should be quite thick. Taste for seasoning.

4 Just before serving, drizzle the remaining olive oil over the dish and garnish with fresh sage leaves.

Cook's Notes
Ask at an Italian delicatessen for fresh pork sausages—salsiccia puro suino. There are many different kinds to choose from and it depends on your personal taste whether you like a mild, herby, or spicy-hot flavor. Whichever you choose, they are bound to have a high meat content because this is how Italians like their sausages. Salsiccie a metro is a long thin sausage that takes its name from the fact that it was traditionally sold by the meter, although nowadays it is more often sold by the kilo. Luganega is one variety of salsiccie a metro that would be suitable for this recipe. Salamelle is another suitable fresh sausage that is sold in links.

Serves 4
Preparation time: 15 minutes, plus overnight soaking
Cooking time: about 1¾ hours

Veal Chops with Savory Butter
Bracioline di Vitello con Burro Piccante

2 garlic cloves

½ cup plus 2 tablespoons butter, diced

3 anchovies, chopped

1 tablespoon chopped parsley

1 lemon

12 veal chops

½ cup dry white wine

6 tablespoons olive oil

½ teaspoon chopped rosemary

salt and pepper

lettuce leaves, to garnish

1 Finely chop 1 garlic clove and mix with the diced butter and anchovies in a small bowl. Add the chopped parsley and season with a squeeze of lemon juice and pepper to taste. Work the mixture together and form it into a ¾ inch diameter cylinder. Wrap in foil and put in the refrigerator to harden.
2 Flatten the veal with a mallet. Make a marinade using the wine, half the oil, rosemary, the other garlic clove (crushed), the remaining lemon juice, and salt and pepper. Marinate the veal for 3 hours.
3 Drain the chops and cook under a hot broiler, using the remaining oil. Serve topped with slices of anchovy butter and lettuce leaves.

Serves 6
Preparation time: 15 minutes, plus marinating
Cooking time: 15 minutes

Veal with Eggplant
Vitello alle Melanzane

4 eggplants, thinly sliced

1 carrot, chopped

1 celery stalk, chopped

½ onion, chopped

1¾ lbs. boned loin of veal

1 cup olive oil

½ teaspoon chopped sage

½ teaspoon chopped rosemary

½ cup wine vinegar

2 garlic cloves, finely chopped

½ teaspoon chopped basil leaves

salt and pepper

1 Cook the eggplants under a hot broiler without adding any fat.
2 Put the carrot, celery, and onion in a pan with the meat, salt, and water to cover. Bring to a boil; simmer gently for 2 hours or until the meat is cooked.
3 Remove and drain the veal. Put 1 tablespoon of the oil in another pan with the sage and rosemary, and lightly brown the veal in it. Pour half the vinegar over it, and leave until it evaporates. Remove the meat and leave to cool.
4 Put a layer of eggplant slices in a shallow dish and season with a little of the garlic, basil, remaining oil and vinegar, and salt and pepper. Continue until the eggplant is used up, and pour any remaining oil over it. Leave to marinate for 1 hour, or longer if convenient.
5 To serve, slice the veal and arrange on a plate alternately with slices of eggplant. Strain the marinade over the dish.

Serves 6
Preparation time: 40 minutes, plus marinating
Cooking time: 2 hours

Tuscan Veal
Vitello alla Toscana

1 Tie the meat up with string, not too tightly, so that it will keep its shape during cooking. Roll it in flour. Melt the butter in a heavy pan over medium heat and brown the meat all over. Add the onion and ham to the pan. Lower the heat and cook for a few minutes until the onion is golden, but not brown.

2 Sprinkle in the wine and simmer until it evaporates. Season with salt and pepper, cover, and cook for about 1½ hours, moistening from time to time with a little stock.

3 At the end of the cooking time, season the meat and cooking juices with the garlic, lemon rind, and nutmeg. Remove the meat.

4 Carve the meat in thick slices and serve with the cooking juices.

Serves 6
Preparation time: 10 minutes
Cooking time: 1¾ hours

2¾ lbs. fillet of veal

¼ cup flour

6 tablespoons butter

I small onion, finely chopped

5 oz. cooked ham, finely chopped

¼ cup red wine

I cup stock

I garlic clove, crushed

grated rind of ½ lemon

¼ teaspoon grated nutmeg

salt and pepper

Roast Pork Loin
Arista di Maiale

1 Make slits in the pork rind with a sharp pointed knife. Fill these with slivers of garlic and pieces of rosemary. Stud with the cloves. Sprinkle with salt and pepper and brush with oil.

2 Put in an oiled roasting pan and cook in a preheated oven, 350°F, for about 1 hour, turning and basting from time to time.

3 Serve either hot in slices or cold with a selection of salads.

Serves 4
Preparation time: 10 minutes
Cooking time: 1 hour

2 lbs. rolled loin of pork

2 garlic cloves, cut into slivers

3 sprigs of rosemary

3 cloves

I tablespoon olive oil

salt and pepper

Loin of Pork with Citrus Fruit

Lonza di Maiale agli Agrumi

4 tablespoons butter

1 small onion, finely chopped

2¾ lbs. loin of pork

1½ tablespoons Marsala wine

juice of 1 orange

juice of 1 lemon

½ cup stock

12 black olives, pitted and chopped

salt and pepper

1 Melt the butter in a large flameproof casserole over medium heat; add the onion and cook until golden, but not brown. Add the loin of pork and brown it on all sides.

2 Add the Marsala and, when this has evaporated, the orange and lemon juice. Season with salt and pepper, cover and cook over low heat for about 1½ hours. Add a little stock from time to time to make sure it does not dry out.

3 Halfway through the cooking time, add the olives to the pork with a little pepper.

4 Serve the pork thinly sliced with the cooking juices poured over, accompanied with roast or mashed potatoes.

Serves 6
Preparation time: 5–10 minutes
Cooking time: 1¾ hours

Rabbit with Mixed Vegetables
Coniglio con Verdure in Salsa

1 Put the rabbit in a bowl with 1 chopped garlic clove, the peppercorns, and vinegar. Cover and leave to marinate for 12 hours, turning the pieces from time to time. Remove and rinse briefly under cold running water and dry on paper towels.

2 Heat the oil in a large deep pan, add the chopped onion, celery, carrot, remaining 2 garlic cloves, and bacon, and cook over low heat until softened. Increase the heat to medium.

3 Dust the rabbit pieces with flour; add to the pan and cook, turning from time to time, until golden on all sides. Season with salt and pepper, moisten with the wine and allow it to evaporate over low heat.

4 Blanch the beans in boiling water for 5 minutes, then drain and chop them into small pieces. Set the chopped beans aside. Add the potatoes to the rabbit. After 5 minutes add the tomatoes and the olives. Cover the pan and simmer for 50 minutes. Add the beans and cook for 10 minutes more.

5 Remove the lid, taste, and adjust the seasoning with salt, if necessary, add 2–3 tablespoons of hot water and continue cooking over moderate heat until the rabbit is tender; about 10 minutes. Shortly before the end of the cooking time, mix in the basil.

6 Transfer to a heated dish and serve hot.

Serves 4
Preparation time: 20 minutes, plus overnight marinating
Cooking time: 1½ hours

- 1 x 3 lb. rabbit, cleaned and jointed
- 3 garlic cloves, finely chopped
- 4 white peppercorns
- 1 cup white wine vinegar
- 4 tablespoons olive oil
- 1 large onion, chopped
- 1 celery stalk, chopped
- 1 carrot, chopped
- 2 oz. bacon, chopped
- 2 tablespoons flour
- ¼ cup red wine
- 5 oz. green beans, ends trimmed
- 3 potatoes, chopped
- 14 oz. can plum tomatoes, drained and chopped
- 2 oz. green olives, pitted and sliced
- 1 bunch of basil, chopped
- salt and pepper

"La prima oliva e oro, la seconda argento, la terza mon val niente.
The best olive is gold, the second silver, the third is worth nothing."

Tuscan Saying

Deviled Chicken
Pollo alla Diavola

2 poussins (very small, very young chickens), spatchcocked (see Cook's Notes)

½ cup olive oil

6 tablespoons lemon juice

2 tablespoons mixed peppercorns, crushed coarsely in a mortar and pestle

coarse sea or rock salt

lemon wedges, to serve

Spit-roasting is one of the most popular methods of cooking in Tuscany, and whole chickens are rotated on spits over charcoal fires, especially in the gardens of open-air restaurants. The method given here is more practical.

1 Put the poussins in a non-metallic dish, and slash them all over with the point of a small sharp knife.

2 Whisk together the oil, lemon juice, and crushed peppercorns, and brush all over the poussins, working the marinade into the cuts in the meat. Cover and leave to marinate for at least 4 hours, preferably overnight, in the refrigerator.

3 Prepare the barbecue and let it burn until the flames have died down and the coals are gray. Sprinkle the skin side of the poussins with salt, then place them skin-side down on the barbecue grill. Cook for 15 minutes, then turn over and cook for 10 minutes more.

4 Remove the poussins from the barbecue grill and cut each bird in half lengthwise with kitchen shears. Serve hot, warm, or cold, with lemon wedges.

Cook's Notes

"Spatchcock" is a culinary term used to describe the opening out and flattening of a whole bird. Its exact origins are unknown, but the most likely explanation is that it comes from "dispatching the cock," an old Irish custom of killing a bird and flattening it so that it roasted quickly over the fire—a measure used by Irish cooks when guests arrived unexpectedly.

Spatchcocking is simple, and a spatchcocked bird will cook in half the time it takes to cook a whole bird. The smaller the bird the easier it is to spatchcock, so poussins and quails are ideal. With the bird breast-side down, cut along each side of the backbone with poultry shears. Discard the backbone, or use it in the stockpot. Put the bird breast-side up on a board and press hard with your hand on the breastbone to break it. To keep the bird flat during cooking, push 2 metal skewers through the bird, one through the wings with the breast in between, the other through the thighs.

This recipe is given its hot or "deviled" flavor by the peppercorns. Some Tuscan recipes use very finely chopped chilies as well.

Serves 4

Preparation time: 10 minutes, plus marinating and time to prepare the barbecue

Cooking time: 25 minutes

Mixed Meat & Poultry Stew

Scottiglia

2 tablespoons olive oil

I carrot, finely chopped

I large onion, finely chopped

I large celery stalk, finely chopped

4 garlic cloves, crushed

2 lbs. mixed meats (see Cook's Notes)

½ bottle red wine, preferably Chianti

14 oz. can chopped Italian plum tomatoes

I sprig of fresh rosemary

salt and pepper

TO FINISH:

4–6 thick slices of country bread

2 garlic cloves, halved

In the old days scottiglia *was a country dish cooked in a communal pot over an open fire. Villagers would gather together in one house and bring with them whatever piece of meat they could spare. Consequently, each* scottiglia *varied according to what was on hand, and this was its charm. This recipe is a modern-day version.*

1 Heat the oil in a large flameproof casserole; add the chopped vegetables and garlic and cook gently, stirring frequently, for about 5 minutes until softened but not colored.

2 Add the pieces of meat and stir to mix with the vegetables, then increase the heat to medium and stir until the meat changes color on all sides. Be careful not to allow the vegetables to burn.

3 Add the wine and tomatoes, the rosemary, and salt and pepper to taste. Bring to a boil, stirring, then cover tightly and cook over the lowest possible heat for 2½–3 hours until the meats are very tender when pierced with a fork. The meat should fall easily from the bones. Taste for seasoning.

4 Just before serving, toast the bread lightly on both sides, then rub one of the sides with the cut side of the garlic. Place the bread, garlic-side up, in warm soup plates. Ladle the stew on top and serve.

Cook's Notes

Old-fashioned recipes for scottiglia *combined many different meats, including game birds, wild boar, and rabbit. Today, a successful* scottiglia *can be made with a mixture of chicken or rabbit, beef, veal, or pork, and even pheasant. Good-quality meat is not as important as variety—the more different types of meat the better, and the more authentic the overall flavor. Fattier cuts are best, together with meat or poultry on the bone: shin of beef or veal, shoulder of pork, chicken thighs, and cut-up rabbit pieces, and pheasant that is not young enough for roasting. Cut the meat, including the bones, into serving pieces roughly equal in size.*

To save time, chop all the vegetables together in a food processor fitted with the metal blade.

Serves 4–6
Preparation time: 20 minutes
Cooking time: 2½–3 hours

Tuscan Meat Rissoles

Polpettine alla Toscana

Polpettine *made with ground beef and grated cheese are really delicious—and very popular in Tuscany. Some Tuscan cooks use the same mixture to make* polpettone, *a large meat loaf which is cut into slices for serving.*

1 Put the bread in a large bowl, add the milk, and squeeze with your fingers to combine the two.
2 Add the ground beef, Parmesan, egg, tomato purée, garlic, sage, and salt and pepper to taste. Mix with your hands until all the ingredients are evenly combined.
3 Break off small pieces of the mixture and form them into 24 oval shapes.
4 Heat about 3 inches of oil in a deep, heavy pan until very hot but not smoking. Add the rissoles in 3 or 4 batches and fry them until browned on all sides. With a slotted spoon, transfer the rissoles to a flameproof casserole .
5 Pour the wine and stock over the rissoles in the casserole and bring to a boil. Season with salt and pepper to taste. Cover and cook over low heat for 20–30 minutes, shaking the pan to baste the rissoles with the cooking liquid from time to time. Serve hot, sprinkled with grated Parmesan.

Cook's Notes
Because polpettine *contain Parmesan cheese, they are very rich and likely to break during cooking. If you have time, chill them, uncovered, in the refrigerator for about 1 hour before cooking—this will help firm them up. Frying them in a good quantity of very hot oil helps seal them at the beginning of cooking, and shaking the pan to coat the* polpettine *in the liquid is better than stirring.*

To make Polpettone, *press the mixture into a loaf pan, then turn it out into the center of a roasting pan. Put the stock, wine, and salt and pepper to taste in a small pan and bring to a boil. Pour over the meat loaf and bake in a preheated oven, 375°F, for 45 minutes, basting several times. Allow the loaf to rest for about 10 minutes before slicing. If you like, boil the cooking liquid on top of the stove until reduced, and serve separately as a gravy.*

Serves 4
Preparation time: 20 minutes
Cooking time: 20 minutes

I thick slice of country bread, crusts removed

2 tablespoons milk

I lb. ground beef

2 oz. Parmesan cheese, grated, plus extra, to serve

I egg, beaten

2 tablespoons tomato purée

2 garlic cloves, crushed

I teaspoon dried sage

vegetable oil, for frying

I cup red wine, preferably Chianti

I cup hot beef stock

salt and pepper

Pan-fried Chicken
Pollo in Padella

3 tablespoons olive oil

1 tablespoon butter

4 chicken breasts, skinned (see Cook's Notes)

¾ cup dry white wine

4–6 fresh sage leaves, roughly chopped

3 tablespoons white wine vinegar

salt and pepper

A quick and simple dish that relies on the quality of its ingredients. Serve it with a salad or a green vegetable such as spinach, French beans, or broccoli.

1 Heat the oil and butter in a large non-stick skillet until foaming. Add the chicken and cook over low to medium heat for 5–7 minutes until golden brown on both sides, turning once.

2 Pour the wine over the chicken, sprinkle the chopped sage over, and season with salt and pepper to taste. Cover and cook over low heat for 15 minutes, spooning the sauce over the chicken from time to time and turning the chicken halfway through cooking.

3 Remove the chicken to warmed dinner plates and keep warm. Add the wine vinegar to the pan juices, increase the heat to high, and stir until the juices are reduced. Spoon the juices over the chicken and serve immediately.

Cook's Notes

Chicken breasts on the bone have the most tender, moist meat, and they are less likely to dry out during cooking. Boneless chicken breasts can be used, but baste them frequently and do not overcook them—the total cooking time should only be 15 minutes.

Serves 4
Preparation time: 5 minutes
Cooking time: 25 minutes

"It would be true to say that Tuscan cooking revolves round the old-fashioned hearth, where pride of place is taken by the grill and the roasting spit."

Ada Boni
Italian Regional Cooking

Roast Lamb
Agnello al Forno

3 lb. leg of lamb

2 garlic cloves, cut lengthwise
    into thin slivers

a few sprigs of fresh rosemary

2 teaspoons dried sage

½ cup olive oil

1 lb. small or baby new potatoes,
    scrubbed

2 red onions, peeled and
    quartered lengthwise

salt and pepper

This is a typical Sunday lunch dish for the family. It is especially popular in spring, with the new season's young lamb.

1 Make deep cuts all over the lamb with a small sharp knife. Insert the garlic slivers and rosemary sprigs into the cuts, then rub the joint all over with the sage, and salt and pepper to taste.

2 Put the lamb in a roasting pan and pour half the oil over it. Roast in a preheated oven, 450°F, for 30 minutes, turning once.

3 Reduce the heat to 375°F. Turn the lamb over again and add the potatoes, onions, and remaining oil. Turn the vegetables to coat them in the oil and sprinkle with salt and pepper to taste. Roast for 1¼ hours or until the lamb is tender, turning the lamb and vegetables 2–3 times.

4 Remove the lamb from the roasting pan and place on a carving board. Cover with foil and leave to rest for 10 minutes. Meanwhile, mix the potatoes and onions with the juices in the pan, then turn them into a warmed serving dish and keep hot.

5 Carve the lamb into thin slices and serve hot, with the potatoes and onions.

Cook's Notes
A gravy can be made with the cooking juices, if you like. Remove the potatoes and onions with a slotted spoon and pour off all but 1–2 tablespoons of the oil from the pan. Place the pan on top of the stove, sprinkle in 2 teaspoons flour, and stir over low heat for 1–2 minutes. Stir in about 1 cup well-flavored stock and a glass or two of red wine, and season to taste with salt and pepper. Bring to a boil and simmer, stirring, until thickened.

Serves 4
Preparation time: 15 minutes
Cooking time: about 1¼ hours

Hunter's Chicken with Polenta

Pollo alla Cacciatora con Polenta

1 Heat the oil in a large skillet and sauté the chicken joints until golden all over, turning occasionally. Remove and keep warm.
2 Add the onion to the pan and cook gently until golden. Add the tomatoes, wine, rosemary, thyme, and salt and pepper. Bring to a boil, stirring, and then reduce the heat to a simmer. Return the chicken to the pan and simmer, covered, for 20–30 minutes until the chicken is cooked.
3 Meanwhile, cook the polenta: bring the water and milk to a boil in a large pan; add the salt, then sprinkle in the polenta in a thin, steady stream, stirring all the time. Cook over medium heat, stirring constantly, for 8 minutes or according to the package instructions. Remove from the heat, beat in the butter until melted, and season with black pepper.
4 Remove the chicken and arrange on a heated serving dish. Blend the flour with the butter and add to the sauce. Bring to a boil, stirring constantly until the sauce thickens slightly. Pour the sauce over the chicken, sprinkle with parsley, and serve with the polenta.

Serves 4
Preparation time: 15 minutes
Cooking time: 30 minutes

4 tablespoons olive oil

I chicken, jointed

I onion, chopped

5 plum tomatoes, skinned and chopped

I cup dry white wine

I sprig of rosemary

I tablespoon chopped fresh thyme

2 tablespoons flour

I tablespoon butter

2 tablespoons chopped parsley

salt and pepper

POLENTA:

3 cups water

I cup milk

I teaspoon salt

8 oz. pre-cooked polenta (see Cook's Notes for Polenta with Wild Boar, page 80)

4 tablespoons butter

vegetables & salads

Tuscany is blessed with an abundance of different vegetables, as a visit to any town or country market will prove. Prized for their superb quality are purple baby artichokes, slender stems of asparagus, young, tender spinach, and white bulbs of fennel, but there is something fresh and new in the market all year round—fava beans and baby artichokes in spring, zucchini and tomatoes in summer, mushrooms and truffles in autumn. Vegetables appear at many different stages of the meal, as antipasti, accompaniments to main courses, even main courses in themselves, and in soups. Beans take center stage, however, for the Tuscans love them, especially the dried white cannellini, which are found in so many soups, salads, and side dishes.

Baby Artichoke Omelette
Tortino alla Toscana

4 baby artichokes (see Cook's Notes)

6 tablespoons olive oil

1 garlic clove, finely chopped

6 eggs

2 tablespoons finely chopped flat-leaf parsley

salt and pepper

Tortino *is the Tuscan version of a thick, flat omelette, and it is traditionally made with globe artichokes, which grow so well in this region. A tortino is similar to a* frittata, *but it is more often baked in the oven rather than on top of the stove, and it is not turned over during cooking or put under the broiler at the finish.*

1 Cut off and discard the tough ends of the artichoke stalks, if any. Pull off any coarse outer leaves, then cut across the tops of the leaves to neaten them. Cut the artichokes in half lengthwise and remove any hairy chokes from the centers. Cut the artichokes lengthwise again, into slices about ¼ inch thick.

2 Heat the oil in a 9 inch skillet with an ovenproof handle. Add the artichoke slices, garlic, and salt and pepper to taste. Cook over low heat, stirring frequently, for 10 minutes or until the artichokes are tender.

3 Beat the eggs and parsley in a bowl, then pour into the pan. Bake in a preheated oven, 350°F, for 20 minutes or until set. Serve hot, sprinkled with plenty of black pepper.

Cook's Notes

The artichokes you need for this recipe are the baby globe artichokes that are so young, sweet, and tender that they could be eaten whole. Purple in color, they are slim and tapered in shape, and are more popular in Italy than the green, bulbous, mature artichokes. Look for them in specialty markets and large supermarkets in the late spring and early summer.

Serves 4

Preparation time: 15 minutes

Cooking time: 20 minutes

Sweet & Sour Glazed Carrots
Carote Agrodolce

2 tablespoons olive oil

1 small onion, finely chopped

¾ lb. carrots, cut into sticks

1 garlic clove, crushed

1½ cups chicken stock

2 teaspoons sugar

1 tablespoon white wine vinegar

4 tablespoons butter

salt and pepper

chopped flat-leaf parsley, to garnish

Glossy and sweet, these carrots are delicious with any roast meat, but they are particularly good with roast chicken.

1 Heat the oil in a saucepan, add the onion, and cook gently, stirring frequently, for 5 minutes until softened but not colored.

2 Add the carrots, garlic, stock, sugar, and season with salt and pepper to taste. Bring to a boil, half cover and simmer for 10 minutes or until the carrots are tender but still retain some bite. Transfer the carrots with a slotted spoon to a warmed serving dish. Cover and keep hot.

3 Add the wine vinegar and half the butter to the liquid in the pan. Simmer over high heat, stirring frequently, for 10 minutes until reduced and glossy. Add the remaining butter and stir until melted, then pour over the carrots and serve immediately, garnished with chopped parsley.

Cook's Notes

Although this recipe is good with young carrots, it is excellent for old, end-of-season carrots that are past their best. The onion and stock give even the most tasteless of carrots flavor, and the butter, sugar, and vinegar form a syrup that coats the carrots in an attractive glaze.

Serves 4
Preparation time: 10 minutes
Cooking time: about 25 minutes

Roast Potatoes with Rosemary
Patate al Rosmarino

Crisp and golden on the outside, tender on the inside, these are the perfect roast potatoes. Tuscans like them with a hint of rosemary, which goes so well with lamb and pork, but you can use a different herb if you prefer, or omit the herbs altogether.

1 Peel the potatoes and cut them into halves or quarters, depending on their size. Place in a saucepan, cover with cold water, and add 1 teaspoon salt. Bring to a boil, half cover and parboil for 10 minutes until just tender.
2 Drain and leave to cool.
3 Put the olive oil and butter in a roasting pan and place in a preheated oven, 375°F, for about 5 minutes until sizzling. Add the potatoes and rosemary, season with salt and pepper to taste, then quickly coat in the oil mixture. Return the pan to the oven and roast the potatoes for 45 minutes or until crisp and golden, turning them twice.
4 With a slotted spoon, transfer the potatoes to a warmed serving dish and spoon over them as much of the olive oil from the pan as you like. Garnish with fresh rosemary sprigs and serve immediately.

Cook's Notes
Good varieties of potato for roasting are the floury King Edward, Maris Piper, and Pentland Squire. If these are parboiled and then left to cool before being added to the sizzling fat, the end result will be perfectly crisp.

Serves 4–6
Preparation time: 15 minutes
Cooking time: 50 minutes

2 lbs. old potatoes (see Cook's Notes)
6 tablespoons olive oil
1 tablespoon butter
2 teaspoons dried rosemary
salt and pepper
fresh rosemary sprigs, to garnish

Beets with Parmesan

Barbabietole alla Parmigiana

4 tablespoons olive oil

2 tablespoons butter

I lb. beets, sliced

3 oz. Parmesan cheese, grated

freshly ground black pepper

1 Heat the oil and butter in a pan until foaming. Put about ⅓ of the sliced beets in an ovenproof dish and drizzle with the oil and butter. Cover with about ⅓ of the grated Parmesan and season to taste.

2 Repeat these layers until all the ingredients are used, then bake in a preheated oven, 400°F, for 15 minutes. Serve hot, straight from the dish.

Cook's Notes

For a simpler dish with baby beets, place the beets in a single layer in an ovenproof dish, pour the hot oil and butter over them, and sprinkle with the Parmesan and pepper. Bake as above.

Serves 6

Preparation time: 10 minutes

Cooking time: 15 minutes

Fennel, Orange & Olive Salad

Insalata di Finocchi, Arance e Olive

4 fennel heads

2 oranges

4 oz. pitted black olives, chopped

5 tablespoons olive oil

2 tablespoons lemon juice

¼ teaspoon cumin seeds

salt and pepper

1 Wash the fennel heads, dry, and cut in half lengthwise. Slice thinly and put in a large salad bowl.

2 Peel the oranges and slice thinly (crosswise); remove pith and seeds and cut each slice into 4. Add to the bowl, with the olives.

3 Mix the oil with the lemon juice in a small bowl; season with a little salt and plenty of pepper. Pour this dressing over the salad and sprinkle the cumin seeds over all. Mix together and leave to rest in a cool place (not the refrigerator) for about 1 hour before serving.

Serves 4

Preparation time: 20 minutes, plus resting

Spinach with Olive Oil & Lemon Dressing
Spinaci, Olio e Limone

1¼ lbs. fresh spinach leaves

2 tablespoons butter

2 garlic cloves, finely chopped

4 tablespoons olive oil

2 tablespoons lemon juice

salt and pepper

This simple vegetable dish is traditionally served as an accompaniment to roast lamb, but it is also very good with roast or broiled chicken. It is more often served lukewarm than piping hot.

1 Wash the spinach in a colander and shake off the excess water. Put the spinach in a large saucepan, sprinkling the layers with salt to taste. Cover the pan and cook over medium heat for 5–7 minutes until the spinach has wilted and is tender, shaking the pan vigorously from time to time.

2 Drain the spinach thoroughly in the colander, then return it to the rinsed-out pan and toss over high heat until any remaining water is gone. Add the butter and garlic and continue tossing until combined with the spinach.

3 Turn the spinach into a serving dish. Drizzle the oil and lemon juice over the spinach, sprinkle with salt and pepper to taste, and serve.

Cook's Notes

The spinach can be cooked and drained several hours in advance, then tossed with the butter and garlic just before serving.

You can use this recipe for frozen leaf spinach. Defrost it first and drain it thoroughly, toss with the butter and garlic. and continue as for fresh spinach.

Serves 6
Preparation time: 5 minutes
Cooking time: about 10 minutes

Stuffed Eggplants
Melanzane Ripiene

1¼ lbs. small round eggplants

½ cup olive oil

I onion, finely chopped

4 anchovy fillets, drained and finely chopped

1¼ lbs. plum tomatoes, deseeded and finely chopped

I heaped tablespoon capers, finely chopped

6 basil leaves, finely chopped

2 oz. Romano cheese, grated

salt and pepper

1 Wash and dry the eggplants, then cut the tops off. Stand the eggplants upright on their ends and then, with a sharp knife, slit the flesh in 1 inch wedge shapes from the top down the sides, making sure that you do not cut through to the base. Sprinkle with salt and leave upside down on a chopping board for 30 minutes to drain off any bitter juices; rinse well.

2 Heat ⅓ of the oil in a shallow pan, add the onion and gently fry until golden brown. Add the anchovies and cook until softened; stir in the tomatoes, capers, and basil; season with pepper to taste. Continue cooking until the sauce has thickened. Remove from the heat and add the Romano cheese.

3 Dry the eggplants on paper towels and put them in an ovenproof dish. Fill with the prepared sauce; drizzle with the remaining oil and put them in a preheated oven, 350°F, for about 30 minutes.

Serves 4
Preparation time: 15 minutes, plus standing
Cooking time: 50 minutes–1 hour

Asparagus Omelette
Frittata di Asparagi

1 lb. young asparagus spears, trimmed

5 eggs

2 tablespoons milk

4 tablespoons finely chopped flat-leaf parsley

2 tablespoons olive oil

1 tablespoon butter

2 tablespoons grated Parmesan cheese

salt and pepper

Every region in Italy seems to have its own version of frittata, *the thick, flat omelette that is cooked on both sides. In Tuscany, vegetable* frittatas *are popular, and this one made with fresh young asparagus is very typical.*

1 Cook the asparagus spears in plenty of salted boiling water for 10 minutes. Drain and refresh under cold running water, then cut into ½ inch lengths.

2 Beat the eggs, milk, and parsley in a bowl and season with salt and pepper to taste. Add the pieces of asparagus and stir to mix.

3 Heat the oil and butter in a 12 inch nonstick skillet until foaming. Pour in the egg mixture and let it settle, then cover the pan and cook over low heat for 10 minutes or until the omelette is almost set.

4 Sprinkle the grated Parmesan evenly over the *frittata,* then put under a preheated broiler for 2–3 minutes until golden brown and set. Serve warm or cold.

Cook's Notes

Try to buy young, thin asparagus spears that only need trimming at the base of the stems. The larger, thicker spears often have very woody stems, and up to a third may need to be trimmed off.

Asparagus pans are tall, and allow you to cook the asparagus spears upright so the stems boil in the water and the delicate tips steam above it. If you are serving asparagus as an antipasto with melted butter, this is the best way to cook it. When boiling asparagus for this recipe, it is not necessary to protect the delicate tips because they are cooked again in the frittata. *The best pan to use is a skillet large enough to allow the asparagus to be cooked lying down.*

Serves 4
Preparation time: 15 minutes
Cooking time: about 25 minutes

Fava Beans with Bacon
Fave Stufate

Pancetta gives fave beans flavor and substance, and it is frequently used in vegetable dishes for this reason. Serve as an accompaniment to roast pork or game.

1 Cook the beans in salted boiling water for 5–6 minutes, or according to the package directions.

2 Meanwhile, put the oil and pancetta in a saucepan and heat gently until the fat runs from the pancetta. Add the onion and garlic and cook gently for about 5 minutes until softened but not colored. Add the tomatoes and their juice, the sage, sugar, and salt and pepper to taste. Bring to a boil, stirring.

3 Drain the beans and add to the tomato sauce, then simmer, uncovered, for 10 minutes, shaking the pan constantly. Taste for seasoning before serving.

Cook's Notes
Fava beans have a very short season in early summer, and freshly picked, young fava beans are delicious cooked in this way. For this recipe you will need about 1 lb. fava beans in their shells, and they will need to be boiled for 15–20 minutes. Once fava beans mature they become woolly and tasteless and develop a tough skin, so don't bother with them—frozen fava beans are good because they are frozen when they are young.

Serves 4–6
Preparation time: 15 minutes
Cooking time: 10 minutes

8 oz. frozen fava beans

2 tablespoons olive oil

4 oz. pancetta, diced small (see Cook's Notes for Chicory Salad, page 118)

1 onion, finely chopped

1 garlic clove, crushed

14 oz. can Italian cherry tomatoes in natural juice

1 sprig of sage

1 teaspoon sugar

salt and pepper

Farmer's Style Cannellini Beans
Fagioli alla Moda del Fattore

1 lb. dried cannellini beans, soaked overnight

1 celery stalk, chopped

2 bay leaves

4 oz. bacon

¼ cup bacon fat

3 tablespoons olive oil

½ onion, finely chopped

1 tablespoon chopped sage leaves

1 sprig of rosemary

1 garlic clove, crushed

3 ripe plum tomatoes, skinned, deseeded and chopped

½ vegetable bouillon cube

2 tablespoons red wine

salt and pepper

1 Put the beans in a large pan with 9 cups water, the celery, and the bay leaves. Bring to a boil and simmer for at least 2 hours until tender.

2 Put the bacon in a small pan with enough water to cover it and boil for 10 minutes. Remove with a slotted spoon and cut into bite-sized pieces.

3 Chop the bacon fat and put it in a shallow pan with the oil. Add the onion, herbs, and garlic; cook over medium heat until the onion is golden.

4 Add the drained cooked beans, mix together, season with salt and pepper to taste and leave for 10 minutes to allow the flavors to mingle.

5 Add the tomatoes to the pan with the boiled bacon. Crumble in the bouillon cube and stir in the wine.

6 Leave the sauce to thicken a little, then taste and adjust the seasoning, if necessary. Serve hot.

Serves 4

Preparation time: 10 minutes, plus overnight soaking
Cooking time: 2¾ hours

Tuna & Olive Salad
Insalata di Tonno e Olive

6 whole carrots

2 potatoes

1 lb. tuna in oil, drained and chopped, oil reserved

4 tablespoons black olives, pitted and halved

2 tablespoons wine vinegar

salt and pepper

4 basil leaves, to garnish

1 Cook the carrots and potatoes in lightly salted boiling water.

2 Dice the potatoes and slice the carrots thinly; put them in a bowl.

3 Add the tuna to the bowl along with the olives.

4 Mix the tuna oil and vinegar together in a screwtop jar, season with salt and pepper to taste; shake well to mix.

5 Pour the dressing over the salad. Mix, and garnish with basil leaves.

Serves 4

Preparation time: 10 minutes
Cooking time: 15 minutes

Chicory Salad
Insalata di Cicoria

2 chicory heads

4 tablespoons olive oil

4 oz. pancetta, diced small

4 oz. hard Romano cheese, grated

1 tablespoon lemon juice

pepper

This decorative side salad is good with plain broiled or barbecued fish or meat. It can also be served as an antipasto, in which case it is best arranged on individual plates.

1 Separate the chicory leaves and wash and dry them carefully. Arrange them, rounded-side down, on a large serving platter.

2 Heat 1 tablespoon of the oil in a non-stick skillet. Add the pancetta and cook over low heat until the fat runs. Increase the heat to medium and cook, stirring constantly, until the pancetta begins to color and crisp. Remove the pan from the heat and transfer the pancetta to paper towels with a slotted spoon. Let the pancetta drain.

3 Sprinkle the pancetta inside the chicory leaves, then sprinkle the Romano over, and pepper to taste.

4 Add the remaining oil and the lemon juice to the pan juices and return the pan to medium heat. Stir until sizzling, then drizzle over the chicory. Serve immediately.

Cook's Notes

Pancetta is a type of cured pork that looks and tastes similar to bacon. It is usually sold sliced from a roll in Italian delicatessens, although it can be bought diced in packages—this is the type you are most likely to find in supermarkets. Pancetta is widely used throughout Italy as a flavoring ingredient, especially in sauces and stuffings, and as a base for casseroles and stews. In this recipe it is used like lardons in a French salad, for its tasty, meaty crunch. It is not difficult to obtain, but you can use unsmoked streaky bacon instead.

Both pancetta and Romano cheese tend to be salty, which is why there is no salt in this recipe.

Serves 4
Preparation time: 20 minutes
Cooking time: about 5 minutes

Spinach Tart
Torta di Spinaci

Serve this vegetable tart for a lunch or light supper with a side salad. Although good warm, it has a better flavor when served cold.

1 Make the pastry: sift the flour, baking powder, and a pinch of salt onto a cold surface. Make a well in the center and put the butter and egg yolk into the well. With your fingertips, gradually work the flour into the butter and egg yolk.

2 Gather the dough together, then roll it out gently into a rough circle on a floured surface. Lift the dough into a 9 inch fluted tart pan with a removable base, and press the pastry into the corners and up the sides with your fingertips. Trim the top edge with a knife, then chill in the refrigerator for 30 minutes.

3 Make the filling: melt the butter in a small pan, add the onion, and cook gently, stirring frequently, for about 5 minutes until softened but not colored. Add the spinach, nutmeg, season to taste with salt and pepper, and stir well to mix. Transfer to a bowl and leave to cool.

4 Prick the bottom of the pastry case with a fork, then line with foil and fill with baking beans. Place on a preheated cookie sheet in a preheated oven, 375°F, and bake for 15 minutes. Remove the foil and beans and set the pastry case aside. Reduce the oven temperature to 325°F.

5 Turn the mascarpone cheese into a large bowl and whisk in the Romano, egg, and egg yolks. Add the cooled spinach and salt and pepper to taste; blend well together, then spoon into the partially baked pastry case. Bake in the oven for 30 minutes, covering the edge of the pastry with foil if it shows signs of overbrowning.

6 Leave the tart to stand for 10–15 minutes before serving.

Cook's Notes
The pastry is rich and sticky, and needs careful handling. See the Cook's Notes for Grandma's Tart on page 134.

Serves 4–6
Preparation time: 30 minutes, plus chilling and cooling
Cooking time: 45 minutes

PASTRY:

1½ cups flour

¼ teaspoon baking powder

½ cup chilled butter, diced

1 egg yolk

salt and pepper

FILLING:

4 tablespoons butter

1 onion, finely chopped

8 oz. frozen leaf spinach, defrosted and well drained

¼ teaspoon grated nutmeg

8 oz. carton mascarpone cheese

2 oz. hard Romano cheese, grated

1 egg

2 egg yolks

Braised Zucchini
Zucchine in Teglia

2 tablespoons olive oil

2 tablespoons butter

1 shallot, finely chopped

6 yellow or green zucchini or a mixture of both, cut into 2 inch sticks

¾ lb. tomatoes

2 tablespoons stock

20 black olives, pitted and halved

¼ teaspoon chopped oregano

1 tablespoon chopped parsley

1 mozzarella cheese, cubed

salt and pepper

1 Heat the oil and butter in a large shallow pan. Add the shallot and cook over low heat until softened. Add the zucchini and cook for a few minutes over high heat, then reduce heat to medium. Add the tomatoes and mash with a fork. Season to taste and leave to cook until the zucchini are tender, adding a little stock if necessary.
2 Add the olives, oregano, and parsley, and scatter the mozzarella cheese over the top. Cover the pan, turn off the heat, and leave to rest for a few minutes before serving.

Serves 4
Preparation time: 10 minutes
Cooking time: 25–30 minutes

Hot Pepper Salad
Insalata di Peperoni Piccanti

4 red peppers

1 sprig of parsley, finely chopped

1 garlic clove, finely chopped

3 oz. tuna in oil, drained

2 hard-boiled eggs, chopped

½ fresh chili, deseeded and finely chopped

2 shallots, finely chopped

2 teaspoons mustard

½ cup olive oil

2 tablespoons wine vinegar

salt

12 stuffed green olives, to garnish

1 Wash and dry the pepper, put on a foil-lined cookie sheet, and cook in a preheated oven, 400°F, for 10 minutes until the skin peels off easily. Cool under cold running water, peel, deseed, and cut into slivers 1½ inches long by ¾ inch wide. Put the slivers in a deep dish.
2 Mix together the parsley, garlic, tuna, eggs, and chili, and add to the pepper slivers.
3 In a small bowl, combine the shallots and the mustard. Gradually add the oil and mix well. Add a pinch of salt and the vinegar, mix again, and pour over the pepper mixture.
4 Garnish with the olives, cover with foil and leave to rest in a cool place for 2 hours before serving.

Serves 4
Preparation time: 15 minutes, plus resting
Cooking time: 10 minutes

Asparagus in Tarragon Sauce
Asparagi con Salsa al Dragoncello

3 lbs. asparagus

1½ oz. tuna in oil, drained and flaked

2 anchovy fillets

¾ cup plus 2 tablespoons olive oil

2 tablespoons dry white wine

2 teaspoons chopped tarragon

2 hard-boiled eggs, yolks and whites separated

½ lemon

salt and white pepper

tarragon sprigs, to garnish

1 Trim off the woody ends from the asparagus and scrape off the tough skin at the lower ends. Rinse under cold running water. Divide into bundles and tie bundles with string. Stand them in a tall pan containing enough salted boiling water to come ⅔ of the way up, and cover the tips with a foil dome. Simmer for 8–18 minutes, depending on the thickness of the asparagus.

2 Meanwhile, prepare the sauce: chop the tuna and anchovies. Put them in a blender or food processor with 2–3 tablespoons of the oil, the wine, and the tarragon.

3 Push the hard-boiled egg yolks through a strainer into a bowl. Add a pinch of salt, then slowly trickle in a few drops of oil and beat with a wooden spoon. Stir in one direction, and add more oil once the first has been absorbed. Continue until all the oil has been used up and the mixture is thick and smooth.

4 Add the mixture to the blender with the lemon juice, season with a pinch of salt if necessary, and a little pepper. Blend briefly to mix the ingredients.

5 Drain the asparagus, and cut off the white ends. Arrange the tips on a heated serving plate and pour the sauce over. Push the hard-boiled egg whites through a strainer and sprinkle them over the asparagus before serving, garnished with sprigs of tarragon.

Serves 4
Preparation time: 10 minutes
Cooking time: 8–18 minutes

"The Florentine, careful and calculating, is a man who knows the measure of all things, and his cooking is an austerely composed play upon essential and unadorned themes."

Marcella Hazan
The Classic Italian Cookbook

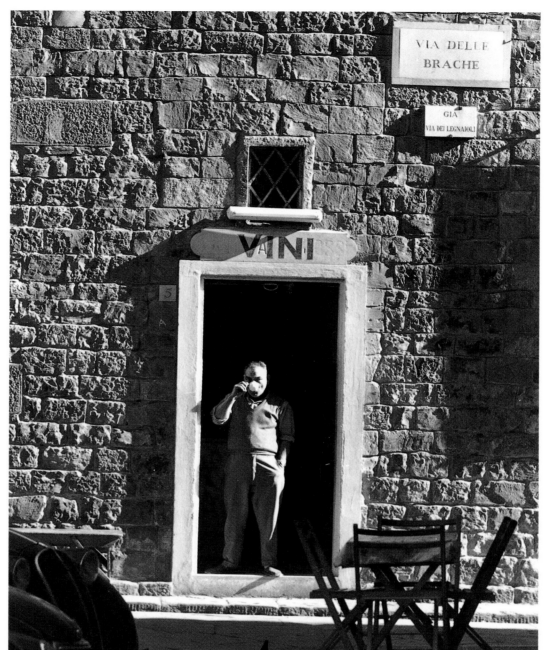

desserts

The most famous Tuscan dessert has to be *Zuccotto*, which some say is named after the cupola on Florence's cathedral—it is shaped like a pumpkin, *zucca* in Italian. *Panforte*, the spicy fruit and nut sweetmeat from Siena, and *cantucci*, hard, sweet cookies, are probably better known outside Italy, but they are more often eaten as a sweet snack with a glass of *vin santo* than as a dessert. On special occasions, pies and tarts are made at home or bought from the local *pasticceria*. The art of pastry making has passed down from the days of Caterina de' Medici, whose pastry chefs were renowned for their skill.

Ice Cream Bombe
Zuccotto

softened butter, for greasing

15–18 *savoiardi* (see Cook's Notes)

about ¾ cup brandy

about 2¼ cups hazelnut ice cream

about 2¼ chocolate ice cream

sifted cocoa powder or
confectioners' sugar, to
decorate

1 Lightly grease the bottom of a 4 cup pudding bowl with the softened butter, then place a circle of waxed paper or parchment paper in the bottom.

2 Check that the *savoiardi* are not too long to fit inside the bowl and trim off the ends if necessary. Pour the brandy into a flat dish.

3 Put one of the *savoiardi* in the brandy, then turn it over several times until it is soaked. Work quickly, taking care that the sponge finger does not break up. Stand the *savoiardi* in the basin with the sugared side facing the basin. Repeat with the remaining *savoiardi* to make a solid lining, working as quickly as possible. Fill in the bottom with broken pieces of *savoiardi,* also soaked.

4 Chill in the refrigerator for at least 30 minutes.

5 Spoon the hazelnut ice cream into the center of the bowl, then spread it up and around the side to completely cover the *savoiardi.* Freeze for about 2 hours until solid.

6 Beat any remaining brandy into the chocolate ice cream, then use to fill the center of the bombe. Level, cover with foil, and freeze.

7 To serve: remove the foil and carefully run a palette knife between the *savoiardi* and the bowl. Invert a chilled serving plate over the bombe, then invert them both. Carefully lift off the bowl and remove the waxed paper circle. Decorate with cocoa powder or confectioners' sugar (see Cook's Notes), and serve immediately.

Cook's Notes

Savoiardi *can be found in packages in Italian delicatessens. They are crisp sponge fingers used in many desserts, but especially* zuccotto *and* tiramisù. *They are firmer than other sponge fingers, and hold their shape better.*

Professionally made zuccotto *has a traditional decoration of confectioners' sugar and cocoa powder striped like a beach ball. It is quite tricky, so you may prefer to simply sift cocoa powder or confectioners' sugar all over the dessert. If you want to make the traditional decoration, it will be easier if you enlist someone to help you—one person should hold the paper while the other does the sifting. Cut a circle of waxed paper to cover the* zuccotto, *fold it into 8 sections, then cut out alternate sections. Position the paper over the* zuccotto *and sift cocoa powder over it. Move the paper around to cover the cocoa powder and sift confectioners' sugar over it.*

Serves 8
Preparation time: 45 minutes, plus chilling and freezing

Neapolitan Curd Tart
Crostata di Ricotta

2 cups flour

pinch of salt

½ cup butter, diced

1 egg yolk

2–3 tablespoons iced water

confectioners' sugar, for dusting

FILLING:

12 oz. ricotta cheese

¼ cup plus 2 tablespoons granulated sugar

3 eggs, well beaten

2 oz. blanched almonds, finely chopped

3 oz. chopped mixed candied peel

rind of of ½ lemon

finely grated rind and juice of ½ orange

¼ teaspoon vanilla extract

1 Sift the flour and salt into a mixing bowl and cut in the butter until the mixture resembles fine breadcrumbs. Mix in the egg yolk and enough iced water to form a soft dough. Knead lightly, and then leave to chill in the refrigerator for 30 minutes. Roll out the pastry to line a 8 inch flan ring. Reserve the pastry trimmings.

2 Next make the filling: rub the ricotta cheese through a strainer into a bowl and then beat in the granulated sugar. Gradually beat in the eggs, and then add the almonds, mixed peel, lemon and orange rind and juice, and the vanilla, beating well between each addition.

3 Pour the ricotta cheese filling into the prepared pastry case and then smooth over the surface.

4 Roll out the reserved pastry trimmings and then, using a fluted roller, cut into thin ½ inch wide strips. Arrange them in a criss-cross pattern over the top of the flan. Bake in the center of a preheated oven, 350°F, for 45–50 minutes, or until set and golden. Cool and serve cold, rather than chilled, dusted with confectioners' sugar.

Serves 6–8
Preparation time: 20 minutes, plus chilling
Cooking time: 45–50 minutes

"Purity is the keynote of Tuscan cooking. And whereas elsewhere in Italy cooking may be said to be a passion, in Tuscany it is an art, as decorous and as formal as that of the great masters of the Florentine school."

Ada Boni
Italian Regional Cooking

Fruit Salad Cake
Macedonia in Torta

1 Prepare the fruit by cutting it into small pieces as you would for an ordinary fruit salad. Place in a large bowl, add the jam, brandy, and wine, stir, and leave to marinate overnight.

2 Sprinkle the yeast over 2–3 tablespoons slightly warmed water and leave until frothy. Melt the butter over very low heat. Sift the flour into a bowl and stir in the melted butter, egg yolks, sugar, yeast mixture, and grated lemon rind. Beat vigorously.

3 Beat the egg whites until they are stiff but not dry. Stir the fruit salad into the dough, then fold in the egg whites. Brush a 10 inch cake pan with oil and dust with flour. Pour in the cake mixture and bake in a preheated oven, 400°F, for 40 minutes. Turn the cake out onto a serving plate and serve warm or cold.

Serves 6
Preparation time: 20 minutes, plus overnight soaking
Cooking time: 40 minutes

I banana

I dessert apple

I peach

8 oz. strawberries

2 pineapple slices

2 tablespoons apricot jam

1½ tablespoons brandy

2 tablespoons white wine

2 tablespoons active dry yeast (2 packets, ¼ ounce each)

½ cup plus 2 tablespoons butter

4¾ cups flour

4 eggs, separated

½ cup pluse 2 tablespoons granulated sugar

rind of I lemon

I teaspoon oil, for greasing

Stuffed Peaches
Pesche Ripiene

1 Cut the peaches in half and remove the pits. With a teaspoon, remove some of the flesh from the centers. Chop this and place in a bowl with the crushed amaretti cookies, liqueur, egg yolks, sugar, almonds, and most of the butter; mix well.

2 Stuff each peach half with this mixture and top with a pat of butter. Put them on an oiled cookie sheet and bake in a preheated oven, 400°F, for 35–40 minutes.

3 Serve warm or cold, sprinkled with icing sugar.

Serves 6
Preparation time: 20 minutes
Cooking time: 35–40 minutes

6 large yellow peaches

4 oz. amaretti cookies, crushed

2 tablespoons amaretto or other liqueur

2 egg yolks

¼ cup plus 2 tablespoons granulated sugar

1½ oz. blanched almonds, finely chopped

¼ cup butter

confectioners' sugar, for decorating

Rags and Tatters
Cenci

2 cups flour

1 teaspoon baking powder

¼ teaspoon salt

2 tablespoons butter

4 tablespoons granulated sugar

finely grated rind of 1 lemon

2 eggs, beaten

3 tablespoons sweet sherry or dry
    white wine (see Cook's Notes)

peanut oil, for deep-frying

confectioners' sugar, to finish

These carnival time fritters are also popular in other regions of Italy, where they are known by different names—in Lazio they are called frappe, *in Naples* chiacchiere. *The Tuscans call them* cenci *because they are made from scraps, or bits and pieces, of dough. They are always made in large quantities because they disappear in minutes, especially when they are still warm and there are children around.*

1 Sift the flour, baking powder, and salt into a bowl, then rub in the butter with your fingertips. Stir in the granulated sugar and lemon rind.

2 Make a well in the center and put in the beaten eggs and sherry or wine. Mix with a wooden spoon until a dough starts to form, then gather the dough together with your hands, adding a little more sherry or wine if the dough is too dry.

3 Turn the dough out onto a floured surface and knead until smooth. Leave to rest in a cool place for 30 minutes.

4 Divide the dough into manageable pieces. Roll out the pieces one at a time on a floured surface until very thin, then cut them into strips measuring about 3 x ¾ inches. Tie each dough strip into a knot.

5 Heat the peanut oil in a deep-fat fryer until 350–375°F, or until a cube of bread browns in 30 seconds. Drop a few *cenci* into the hot oil and deep-fry for 1–2 minutes until golden and crisp. Lift out with a slotted spoon and drain on paper towels while deep-frying the remainder. Sift confectioners' sugar over the *cenci* while they are still warm.

Cook's Notes

Traditional Tuscan recipes flavor the dough with acquavite, *a distilled raw spirit, or with* vin santo, *a dessert wine from the region, which can be bought at Italian delicatessens. Sweet sherry or white wine are the best substitutes if you do not have the real thing.*

Makes about 50
Preparation time: 20 minutes, plus resting
Cooking time: 10–20 minutes

Rice Tart
Torta di Riso

PASTRY:

1½ cups flour

¼ teaspoon baking powder

pinch of salt

¼ cup granulated sugar

finely grated rind of 1 lemon

½ cup chilled butter, diced

1 egg yolk

FILLING:

1¾ cups milk

2½ oz. arborio rice

finely grated rind of 1 lemon

1 vanilla pod, split (see Cook's Notes)

½ cup unsalted butter, softened

¼ cup granulated sugar

4 oz. candied peel, chopped

2 eggs, separated

6 tablespoons apricot jam (see Cook's Notes)

1 Make the pastry: sift the flour, baking powder, and salt onto a cold surface and stir in the sugar and lemon rind. Make a well in the center and put the butter and egg yolk into the well. With your fingertips, gradually work the flour into the butter and egg yolk. Gather the dough together, then press it into a 9 inch fluted tart pan with a removable base. Chill for 30 minutes.

2 Prick the bottom of the pastry case all over with a fork, then line with foil and fill with baking beans. Place on a preheated cookie sheet in a preheated oven, 375°F, and bake for 15 minutes. Remove the foil and beans and set the pastry case aside. Reduce the heat to 325°F.

3 Make the filling: put the milk, rice, lemon rind and vanilla in a heavy saucepan and bring to a boil. Cook over low heat, stirring, for 30 minutes or until the rice is very soft and all the milk is absorbed. Cover the pan and leave until completely cold and stiff.

4 Beat the butter and sugar together in a bowl, then beat in the peel and egg yolks. Remove the vanilla from the rice, then beat the rice into the peel mixture a little at a time, until evenly mixed.

5 Whisk the egg whites until stiff, then fold into the filling with a large metal spoon until evenly incorporated.

6 Spread about half of the apricot jam over the bottom of the partially baked pastry case, then spoon in the filling and level the top.

7 Bake for 25 minutes or until the filling is set in the center. Cover the edge of the pastry with foil if it shows signs of overbrowning.

8 Leave the tart to cool in the pan for 10 minutes, then brush with the remaining jam. Leave until completely cold, then unmold before serving.

Cook's Notes

Vanilla pods are available at supermarkets and delicatessens. They need to be split lengthwise with a sharp knife before use, to release their flavor. After use, rinse the pod under cold running water and wipe dry, then keep it in an airtight container and use it again.

To make the apricot jam easier to spread, warm it gently in a small heavy saucepan, then work it through a strainer with a metal spoon.

Serves 4–6
Preparation time: 40 minutes, plus chilling
Cooking time: 40 minutes

Spicy Fruit & Nut Sweetmeat
Panforte di Siena

At Christmas the familiar octagonal boxes of panforte *can be seen in* pasticcerie *all over Italy, but especially in the town of Siena where this unusual delicacy is made. With its chewy texture dense with candied peel, nuts, and honey, and its spicy flavor, it is quite unique. The usual custom is to eat it with espresso coffee or a glass of sweet* vin santo, *at teatime.*

1 Brush the inside of a 8 inch springform cake pan lightly with softened butter, then place a circle of waxed paper or parchment paper over the base. Set aside.

2 Spread the hazelnuts out on a cookie sheet. Place in a preheated oven, 350°F, for 7–10 minutes until the nuts are toasted. Remove the nuts from the oven and reduce the heat to 300°F.

3 Pour the hazelnuts into the center of a clean dish towel and wrap the towel tightly around them. Leave to steam in the towel for just a few minutes.

4 Rub the nuts in the towel to remove their skins, then coarsely chop them and the candied peel.

5 Place the nuts and peel in a bowl together with the flour, cocoa powder, and spices. Stir well to mix, then set aside.

6 Put the sugar, honey, and butter in a small heavy saucepan and stir over low heat until melted. Increase the heat to high and boil the mixture without stirring for 3 minutes. Pour immediately into the nut mixture and stir to mix, then turn the mixture out onto the work surface and knead to a pliable dough with your hands.

7 Press the mixture into the prepared pan to form a thin, even layer, then bake for 35 minutes. Leave to cool and harden in the pan for about 30 minutes, then remove the side of the pan and lift the *panforte* off the base, leaving the paper behind. Sprinkle with confectioners' sugar and cut into thin wedges to serve.

Serves 8–10
Preparation time: about 1 hour
Cooking time: 35 minutes

2 tablespoons unsalted butter, plus extra for greasing

7 oz. shelled hazelnuts

4 oz. candied peel

¼ cup flour

¼ cup cocoa powder

large pinch each of ground cinnamon and coriander

½ cup granulated sugar

½ cup honey

confectioners' sugar, to finish

Grandma's Tart
Torta della Nonna

PASTRY:

1½ cups flour

¼ teaspoon baking powder

pinch of salt

¼ cup plus one tablespoon
    granulated sugar

finely grated rind of 1 lemon

½ cup chilled butter, diced

1 egg yolk

FILLING:

2 eggs

2 egg yolks

¼ cup granulated sugar

4 teaspoons corn flour (available in
    health food stores)

finely grated rind of 1 lemon

1 cup milk

1 cup heavy cream

confectioners' sugar, to finish

1 Make the pastry: sift the flour, baking powder, and salt onto a cold surface and stir in the sugar and lemon rind. Make a well in the center and put the butter and egg yolk into the well. With your fingertips, gradually work the flour into the butter and egg yolk. Gather the dough together, then roll it out gently into a rough circle on a floured surface. Lift the pastry into a 9 inch fluted tart pan with a removable base and press it into the corners and up the sides with your fingertips. Trim the top edge with a knife, then chill in the refrigerator for 30 minutes.

2 Prick the bottom of the pastry case all over with a fork, then line with foil and fill with baking beans. Place on a preheated cookie sheet in a preheated oven, 375°F, and bake for 15 minutes. Remove the foil and beans and set the pastry case aside, still on the cookie sheet. Reduce the oven heat to 325°F.

3 Make the filling: put the eggs, egg yolks, sugar, corn flour, and lemon rind in a bowl and whisk well to mix. Heat the milk and cream in a heavy saucepan until just below boiling point, then pour into the egg mixture, whisking all the time. Return to the pan and cook over low heat until thickened, stirring constantly.

4 Pour the custard into the partially baked pastry case and bake for 30 minutes or until the filling is just set.

5 Leave the tart until lukewarm in the tart pan, then place on a serving platter. Serve warm or cold, with confectioners' sugar sifted over the top.

Cook's Notes

Adding corn flour to the egg custard is not traditional, but it does help prevent the custard from curdling. Try to keep the heat under the pan low so that the custard does not become too hot.

The pastry dough is very rich and difficult to roll out, which is why it is pressed into the pan with the fingers. Do not worry that it is sticky; it will firm up in the refrigerator and you will appreciate its rich taste.

Serves 6
Preparation time: 40 minutes, plus chilling
Cooking time: 45 minutes

Raspberry Meringue
Meringata ai Lamponi

3 egg whites

I cup confectioners' sugar

I cup heavy cream

I¼ lb. fresh raspberries

1 Beat the egg whites until stiff. Gently fold in all but 2 tablespoons of the confectioners' sugar; beat again until smooth and standing in peaks.
2 Line 2 cookie sheets with parchment paper. Pipe half the meringue mixture onto each sheet in the shape of a large disc. Bake in a preheated oven, 325°F, for about 1 hour until dry and light. Leave to cool.
3 Whip the cream and sweeten it with the remaining confectioners' sugar. Add a few of the raspberries, folding them in gently.
4 Place one meringue on a large dish. Pile on the whipped cream and top with the second meringue. Chill for 1 hour.
5 Meanwhile, purée the remaining raspberries. Pour the purée into a sauceboat and serve separately with the meringue.

Serves 6
Preparation time: 30 minutes, plus cooling and chilling
Cooking time: 1 hour

Deep-fried Amaretti
Frittelline agli Amaretti

¾ cup flour, sifted

8 oz. ricotta cheese, strained

4 oz. amaretti cookies, crushed

½ cup instant chocolate milk powder

4 tablespoons granulated sugar

1½ tablespoons amaretto liqueur

3 eggs

I egg yolk

2 oz. fine dried breadcrumbs

peanut oil, for deep-frying

extra granulated sugar, to serve

1 Work the flour into the ricotta. Add the crushed amaretti cookies with the chocolate milk powder, sugar, and liqueur. Mix in 2 whole eggs and 1 egg yolk—this stage can be done in a food processor.
2 When a thick paste is obtained (if the mixture is too wet add a little more flour), form into little flattened rounds. Beat the remaining egg and mix with 2–3 tablespoons cold water. Dip the flattened rounds into the egg mixture and then in the breadcrumbs.
3 Heat plenty of oil in a large deep pan. When the oil is very hot, add the little cakes in batches and fry until golden on both sides. Drain on paper towels. Sprinkle with granulated sugar and serve.

Serves 6
Preparation time: 20 minutes
Cooking time: 15 minutes

Chestnut Bombe
Monte Bianco

The origins of this dessert are obscure, apart from the fact that it takes its name from Mont Blanc in the French Alps. Cooks all over Italy make Monte Bianco *for special occasions, and Tuscans are no exception.*

1 Put the chestnuts and rum in a food processor fitted with the metal blade and process to a purée. Transfer the purée to a bowl.
2 Put the water, sugar, and fennel seeds in a small heavy saucepan and heat gently until the sugar has dissolved. Increase the heat and boil the liquid for about 5 minutes until reduced and syrupy. Strain the syrup into the chestnuts and beat well to mix, then taste and beat in more rum and sugar if you like.
3 Form the chestnut purée into a cone shape on a serving plate and chill in the refrigerator for 1–2 hours.
4 Whip the cream and confectioners' sugar until the cream holds its shape, then swirl all over the chestnut mound with a palette knife. Chill in the refrigerator until serving time.

Cook's Notes
In Tuscany there are plenty of fresh chestnuts to make this dessert, but they are very tricky to peel and skin, and many modern cooks prefer the convenience of canned chestnuts, especially for a dinner party dessert like this one. Packed in brine, they are available in supermarkets and delicatessens. Do not be tempted to use canned chestnut purée, because it is already sweetened. It is much better to flavor the purée yourself.

In Italy a hand-operated food mill or mouli would be used to purée the chestnuts, and you can use one if you have one. A food mill gives a slightly coarser result than a food processor.

Serves 6
Preparation time: 30 minutes, plus chilling

3 x 8 oz. cans chestnuts, drained

4 tablespoons rum

½ cup water

4 tablespoons sugar

2 tablespoons fennel seeds

1 cup heavy cream

2 tablespoons confectioners' sugar

*"In Santa Croce's holy precincts lie
Ashes which make it holier, dust which is
Even in itself an immortality."*

Lord Byron
Childe Harold's Pilgrimage

Sweet Bread
Stiacciata Unta

about 4 cups bread flour

½ teaspoon salt

1 packet of rapid-action dry yeast

½ cup granulated sugar

½ cup unsalted butter, at room
temperature

2 egg yolks

¾ cup plus 2 tablespoons tepid
water

¼ cup orange juice

finely grated rind of 2 large
oranges

TO FINISH:

¼ cup unsalted butter, softened

confectioners' sugar

*This Florentine bread is a modern interpretation of an ancient recipe.
Stiacciata means "squashed," referring to the fact that the bread is flat.
It is eaten at carnival time in February.*

1 Brush the inside of a 12 x 10 inch roasting pan lightly with oil.
Sift the flour and salt into a warmed large bowl, stir in the yeast and
sugar, then rub in the butter with your fingertips. Stir in the egg
yolks with a fork and then make a well in the center.
2 Mix the water and orange juice with the orange rind. Gradually
work the liquid into the flour mixture, then turn out onto a floured
surface and knead for about 10 minutes until smooth and elastic.
The dough is quite sticky, so work a little more flour into it as you
knead, but take care not to add too much or the finished bread will
be dry and tough.
3 Turn the dough into the pan and stretch and pull it to fit the pan
evenly. Cover with oiled plastic wrap. Leave to rise in a warm place
for 1–1½ hours or until the dough has risen to about twice its
original height. Remove the plastic wrap.
4 Bake in a preheated oven, 350°F, for 30–35 minutes until golden
brown. Remove the *stiacciata* from the oven, brush with the softened
butter, and sift confectioners' sugar liberally all over the top. Leave to
cool in the pan for 20–30 minutes, then cut into rectangles and sift
more confectioners' sugar over them if you like. Serve warm.

Cook's Notes
*Traditional recipes for this bread used fresh yeast. Rapid-action dry yeast is
a powder which is stirred directly into the flour. It contains ascorbic acid
(vitamin C), which accelerates the action of the yeast. Rapid-action dry
yeast eliminates the process of starting the yeast at the beginning of bread-
making, and the dough only needs one rising, so it is much quicker than
fresh yeast or active dry yeast granules. Look for it in packets in the baking
sections of supermarkets.*

Makes 16 rectangles
Preparation time: 30 minutes, plus rising
Cooking time: 30–35 minutes

glossary

Agrodolce: sour-sweet. Describes the flavor of a sauce containing both vinegar and sugar. Most often used with fish or meat; sometimes raisins are included.

Al dente: to the tooth. Cooking term used for pasta and vegetables that still retain some bite after cooking.

Amaretti: almond macaroons. The most famous variety come paper-wrapped from Saronno in Lombardy.

Amaretto: a liqueur made from almonds or apricot kernels. Originated in Saronno, Lombardy.

Arborio: round-grain rice with high starch content used for making risotto.

Borlotti, *see Fagioli.*

Bruschetta: toasted country bread with olive oil and garlic. *Fettunta* is the Tuscan version, which is sometimes untoasted.

Cacciatora, alla: hunter's style. Describes dishes made with a sauce of tomatoes, onions, garlic, and mushrooms. Most often used with chicken.

Cannellini, *see Fagioli.*

Cinghiale: wild boar.

Crescentine: squares of pasta dough that are deep-fried in oil. A Tuscan speciality.

Crespelle: pancakes. Usually stuffed and rolled, coated in béchamel sauce and baked au gratin.

Crostini: croutons. Can be a garnish for soups, but in Tuscany they are toasted or fried rounds of country bread which are used as a base for various antipasti toppings. *Crostini di Milza e Fegatini* are the most famous.

Diavola, alla: deviled. Two meanings —either a chicken split, flattened, and broiled or barbecued, or a dish with a spicy sauce containing chilies or chili powder.

Dolce: sweet. Used to describe the dessert course of a meal, or simply "sweet things" such as pastries and cakes.

Dolcelatte, *see Gorgonzola.*

Fagioli: beans, usually dried. Borlotti are speckled pink or red, and the same shape as red kidney beans. Cannellini are small and white, similar to haricot beans.

Fave: fava beans.

Fegato: liver. *Fegatini di pollo* are chicken livers.

Fettunta, *see Bruschetta.*

Fiorentina, alla: Florentine-style. Correctly used, this term describes dishes from Florence, but it is often mistakenly used to describe dishes containing spinach.

Fontina: a mountain cheese with a sweet, nutty flavor, from *Valle d'Aosta* in north-western Italy. Although a table cheese, it has very good melting qualities in cooking.

Forno, al: in the oven. Describes dishes that are oven-baked.

Funghi: mushrooms. See *Porcini.*

Gnocchi: dumplings. Can be made of flour or potato dough.

Gorgonzola: a blue-veined cheese with a creamy texture from Lombardy. Dolcelatte is a milder version.

Insalata: salad.

Involtini: slices of meat, poultry, or fish wrapped around a stuffing.

Livornese, alla: from the town of Livorno, on the coast of the Ligurian Sea in northern Tuscany. Most often used to describe fish and shellfish dishes from there.

Marinara, alla: sailor-style. Describes dishes containing fish or shellfish.

Marsala: a fortified dessert wine from the town of Marsala in Sicily. Can be dry or sweet. Often used in cooking.

Mascarpone: a fresh creamy cheese that is high in fat. Used in sauce making and desserts, and eaten on its own, sometimes flavored with fruit, sugar, and liqueur.

Mozzarella: made from buffalo or cow's milk, or a mixture of the two. Fresh varieties are moist and dripping with whey; packaged mozzarella can be tasteless and rubbery. Eaten uncooked in salads, especially with tomatoes, but perhaps best known for its melting qualities on top of pizza.

Nonna, della: grandmother-style. Used to describe simple and traditional dishes.

Pane di campagna: country bread. A generic term for a rustic loaf, often coarse-textured. Individual names differ according to regional origin. A saltless bread, called *pane sciocco*, is traditional in Tuscany.

Pancetta: belly of pork cured with salt and spices. Sold sliced, mainly for use as a flavoring ingredient in *soffritto* (see below).

Pappardelle: wide egg ribbon noodles with frilly edges. A Tuscan specialty.

Parmigiano-Reggiano: Parmesan cheese. A hard, grainy cheese. Only cheeses from around the town of Parma in Emilia-Romagna can have the official stamp *"parmigiano-reggiano"* on their rinds. Young Parmesan is a good table cheese; mature varieties are hard, and best for grating and shaving curls.

Passata: strained tomatoes sold in thick, concentrated form in bottles and cans. Used in sauces, soups, and stews.

Pasta frolla: shortcrust pastry, often made with sugar and used for sweet tarts.

Penne: quills. Short tubes of pasta, either plain or ridged (*penne rigate*).

Pesto: a sauce made from basil, garlic, olive oil, Parmesan cheese, and pine nuts, which originated in Liguria. Used with pasta, and as a topping for soups and *crostini*.

Pizzaiola, alla: pizza-style. A term used to describe a dish from the Campania region in southern Italy. Tomatoes are the common ingredient—black olives, capers, anchovies, garlic, oregano, and mozzarella may also be included, like the topping for a traditional Neapolitan pizza.

Polenta: yellow cornmeal or maize flour popular in northern Italy. Can be served "wet," that is, boiled and mixed with butter and sometimes cheese, or cut into shapes after boiling and cooling, then charbroiled, fried, or baked.

Polpettine: little meatball. *Polpettone* is the word for meat loaf, which is traditionally made with ground beef and cheese in Tuscany.

Porcini: ceps or *boletus* mushrooms, very popular in Italian cooking. Although they are used fresh, dried are more common for sauces, stuffings, and stews, etc. They need to be rehydrated in warm water before use, then drained and squeezed to extract liquid. The soaking liquid is a good flavoring.

Prosciutto: ham. The best-known outside Italy is *prosciutto di Parma* or Parma ham, from around the town of Parma in Emilia-Romagna. *Prosciutto Tòscano* is slightly saltier in flavor.

Ragù: meat sauce. The most famous is ragù Bolognese, a rich ground-beef sauce named after the town of Bologna, the capital of Emilia-Romagna. The Tuscan version contains chicken livers.

Ricotta: a soft, very white, fresh cheese made from the "re-cooked" whey of sheep's or cow's milk. Can be eaten fresh, but is used extensively in cooking, especially in desserts and baking. Sold loose, cut from a round cake shape, or in plastic tubs.

Riso: rice. As popular in northern Italy as pasta is in the south. Most often cooked as risotto and served then as a first course on its own. Round-grain rice such as arborio is used—it absorbs stock gradually and swells up to become creamy in consistency.

Romano: a country cheese that can be soft and mild, but is more usually hard and sharp. It is similar to Parmesan, but often sharper and saltier, it is often used grated in cooking.

Rucola: arugula or roquette. An aromatic salad green with a peppery bite.

Rustica, alla: rustic. A term used to describe a traditional, country dish.

Salame: salami. Salt-cured sausages which differ enormously from one region to another, and even within regions. Mostly used thinly sliced as an antipasto, but also sometimes diced and used for flavor in cooking, especially if they are spicy, peppery, or garlicky.

Salsa: sauce. Usually uncooked.

Salsiccia: fresh sausage, usually long and thin and made of pork. There are numerous different varieties, coarse and fine, mild and spicy. *Salsiccia a metro*—sausage by the meter—is cut and sold by the kilogram.

Saporita: tasty. From the word *sapore*, meaning taste or flavor.

Sfogliata: puff or flaky pastry.

Soffritto: A flavoring base for sauces, stuffing, soups, and stews. Chopped onion, celery, garlic, and carrot are commonly used, fried gently in olive oil. Diced pancetta (see above) is sometimes added for extra flavor.

Sugo: sauce. Usually cooked.

Torta: tart. Can be savory or sweet. Also used to describe a pie or a cake.

Toscana, alla: Tuscan-style.

Uccelletto, all': cooked on skewers and/or flavored with sage. From the word *uccelletti* for little birds, such as thrushes and larks, which were traditionally cooked on spits over the fire and flavored with fresh sage leaves.

index

Quotations

D.H. Lawrence, *Cypresses*, p. 5
Montaigne, *Journal du Voyage en Italie*, p. 5
Traditional Tuscan saying, p. 6
Elizabeth Barrett Browning, *Complete Verse*, p. 12
Elizabeth David, *Tuscan Food*, p. 16
Traditional Florentine saying, p. 18
Anonymous traditional rhyme, p. 38
D.H. Lawrence, *Etruscan Places*, p. 43
Elizabeth Barrett Browning, *Complete Verse*, p. 44
Ada Boni, *Italian Regional Cooking*, p. 52
D.H. Lawrence, *Etruscan Places*, p. 57
Lord Byron, *Childe Harold's Pilgrimage*, p. 72
D.H. Lawrence, *Etruscan Places*, p. 76
Folgore da San Gemigano, translated by Dante Gabriel Rossetti, p. 83
Elizabeth David, *Tuscan Food*, p. 84
Alfred Lord Tennyson, *The Daisy*, p. 86
Traditional Tuscan saying, p. 95
Ada Boni, Italian Regional Cooking p100
Marcella Hazan, The Classic Italian Cookbook p122
Ada Boni, *Italian Regional Cooking*, p. 128
Lord Byron, *Childe Harold's Pilgrimage*, p. 137